NOT FROM HERE

ALSO BY ALLAN G. JOHNSON

NONFICTION

The Gender Knot

The Forest and the Trees

Privilege, Power, and Difference

The Blackwell Dictionary of Sociology

FICTION

The First Thing and the Last

Nothing Left to Lose

NOT FROM HERE

A Memoir

ALLAN G. JOHNSON

TEMPLE UNIVERSITY PRESS
Philadelphia • Rome • Tokyo

TEMPLE UNIVERSITY PRESS
Philadelphia, Pennsylvania 19122
www.temple.edu/tempress

Published 2015

Library of Congress Cataloging-in-Publication Data

Johnson, Allan G.
Not from here : a memoir / Allan G. Johnson.
pages cm
ISBN 978-1-4399-1245-4 (cloth : alkaline paper) — ISBN 978-1-4399-1247-8 (e-book) 1. Johnson, Allan G.—Travel—Middle West. 2. Johnson, Allan G.—Travel—Great Plains. 3. Johnson, Allan G.—Family. 4. Johnson, Valdemar N. L., 1912–2005—Death and burial. 5. Fathers and sons—United States. 6. Men, White—United States—Biography. 7. Belonging (Social psychology)—United States. 8. Ethnicity—United States—Psychological aspects. 9. Indians, Treatment of—United States. 10. United States—Race relations. I. Title.
CT275.J6295A3 2015
306.874'2—dc23

2014043114

∞ The paper used in this publication meets the requirements of the American National Standard for Information Sciences—Permanence of Paper for Printed Library Materials, ANSI Z39.48-1992

Printed in the United States of America

9 8 7 6 5 4 3 2 1

For my father

Pierre
S.D.
(Grasslands)
Pine
Ridge
Rosebud
W
S

Watertown
S.D.

St. Paul
MN

Hayti
S.D.

Lower
Sioux — Mankato

Wells
MN

Decorah
IA

E.

Thor
IA

Hardanger
4,000 miles

PROLOGUE

I began life with a special relation to basements and cellars. When I was a boy in Washington, D.C., we lived in a place called McLean Gardens, a housing project that had been built during World War II. The buildings were connected through a labyrinth of basement corridors broken into sections by massive fire doors that closed themselves to the clanking of counterweights on chains pulling up, like the drawbridge Errol Flynn's Robin Hood scales in pursuit of his beloved in the clutches of the wicked prince and the sheriff of Nottingham.

Each apartment was connected to the basement by a stairwell running off the kitchen, and it was my job after dinner to take the garbage down three flights of stairs and put it in a can at the bottom. I will never forget the sound of the apartment door closing behind me and the feeling of descent as I went down and down on my skinny five-year-old legs, the bag clutched in my hand, fear doing flip-flops in my belly, alert to the sound of clanking chains, afraid of something—just what, I didn't know, except that it was going to reach out and grab hold of me before I had a chance to get back up the stairs. And I will never forget the feeling of release the moment I dropped the bag into the can and slammed down the lid and raced back up to the safety of the light and my family and the door closing behind me.

Another basement was in the house of my great-aunt Alice Bailey. She lived for many years in Massachusetts with her sister, Bullah, who helped found the Little Theater movement and corresponded with Bernard Shaw about producing one of his plays. Bullah was married to Uncle Ned, an inventive Yankee who made a cannon that he liked to shoot off on Sunday mornings just to rouse the neighborhood and who built a giant wooden bird perched on a pole, whose wings would flap in the wind.

While my mother visited with Aunt Alice in the kitchen, I did what children do and wandered around looking for things to get into. When I happened to open a door off the kitchen, the dank smell of an ancient basement drifted up the stairs and took hold of some longing deep inside me, drawing me down into the darkness, which, for some reason I can't recall, I did not fear. I remember nothing of that place except the smell, the memory of which still touches in me a deep sense of rootedness in the earth, timeless and silent.

Well, not quite nothing. There was also what I saw on the bedside table in Aunt Bullah and Uncle Ned's room. There was a book, which I remember only as being authored by J. Edgar Hoover and having something about communism in the title. And beside it was the largest revolver I've ever seen, and I could tell, leaning down so my cheek almost rested on the table, that it was loaded.

It was my fate to be born a white man in the United States, a house of endless rooms described to me from before the time when I could understand the words as a matchless home to light and industry, equality, courage, and liberty, and noble striving for the freedom to be who you are, all of which coalesces in the tears that come whenever I hear *Oh, beautiful, for spacious skies, for amber waves of grain. . . . America. . . .*

A flawed house, to be sure, being full of human beings with a tendency to overreach and dark times when the worst comes out, but one in which we tell ourselves and the world that we are always forging ahead with the finest of intentions and are destined to be the envy of the world and ultimately find redemption in the relentless pursuit of what is just and good.

It was my fate to be enfolded in this house's vision of itself that I would love for many years as the place where I was from and, through that, know who I was and where I belonged.

I did not know for a long, long time about the nether regions of this enormous house, deep below the light and air in the foundation on which it rests, the thing that holds it up, where all the artifacts and memories that are unwanted and shunned are cast out and hidden away to be forgotten as if they never were.

It was also my fate to spend the first six years of my life in Washington, D.C., the capital of this house with endless rooms. I sailed toy boats on the Reflecting Pool in front of the Lincoln Memorial and listened to the Marine Band give Sunday concerts on the Capitol steps, and my father took me to visit Arlington Cemetery and the Tomb of the Unknown Soldier. It was in this city that I first came to love the idea of America long before I knew how much of it was built on the slave labor of human beings kidnapped from Africa. I did not know this until many decades after leaving that shining city, and only then because of my destiny, which, to judge from the course of my life as I look back upon it, has been to go down into those nether regions and sit and listen and feel the presence of all the things this house seems organized to forget—and then to come back into the light and remember and speak and write it all down.

I cannot change my fate, it being fixed in the past, in whatever I came in with, born into a particular time and place. But destiny, the trajectory of fate through the living of my life, what it is that I came here to do, may or may not come to pass, depending on many things I cannot control but a few that I can.

It has been my destiny to go down into the cellar of this nation's history and then return. In doing that, I have had to become familiar with dark nights of the soul, to grow accustomed to the belly of the whale. There have been many times when I wished for something else, but destiny is destiny and fate is fate and, besides, I have learned that if you hang on long enough, there always comes a moment when the whale gives you up and spits you out. And for that moment, you must be ready.

NOT FROM HERE

When my father was very old, I asked him where he wanted his ashes to be scattered when he was gone. As far as I could tell, on this subject, he simply had no feeling at all.

"It doesn't matter," he said. "Makes no difference to me at all."

It startled me how little time he took to consider, just enough to gather himself into a shrug, to look away, drawing in a breath.

No bitterness or despair, no sadness or regret.

He was perfectly content.

I have come to wish that I had asked for something more.

My father died of congestive heart disease and kidney failure on December 5, 2005. He was ninety-three years old and had lived what he described as a long and happy life. I spent his last night alone with him in the hospital in Port Angeles, Washington, the window in his room affording a view through lightly falling snow of the Strait of Juan DeFuca. When I wasn't sleeping on the cot the nursing staff brought in, I sat beside his bed in silence or carrying on a one-sided conversation or mangling Norwegian songs he'd taught to us as children. He was unconscious when I arrived and stayed that way to the end, but I'm sure he knew that I was there, had waited for me, in fact. I have no doubt because of how easily it came to me what to say throughout the long hours of the night, and I have no doubt because of how he murmured when I stroked his forehead and how agitated he became when I stopped, and I have no doubt because, well, there are just some things about which you have no doubt.

A few days after he died, I went to the funeral home to pick up his ashes. They came in three brown plastic boxes, one each for me, my brother, and my sister, with labels on the front listing the name and address of the funeral home and below that:

This package contains the cremated body of
Valdemar N. L. Johnson
Cremated December 7, 2005, ID Number 20051912
Olympic Cremation Association

One side bore a label warning NOT SUITABLE FOR MAILING OR LONG-TERM STORAGE, making it clear this was not to be his final resting place. And yet, here it is, the little box on the table beside me now, more than two years later, the cover dusty from sitting on a shelf in the laundry room. Nora has told me more than once that it is no proper place for him to be, and yet, from what my father told me when I asked, one is no better than another. I know she's right, but something keeps me from moving him until this morning, taking him down to open him up. Maybe he has thought it over.

There is a rubber band around the box, although just why I've no idea, since it opens from the top. It takes a screwdriver to get the lid off. Inside is a large wad of white batting and beneath that a clear plastic bag of what remains of my father. He is reduced to a grainy powder, olive drab, and the texture through the plastic reveals some tiny rough pieces, what I imagine is left from the grinding of his bones. The smooth plastic of the bag reflects the morning light coming through the window. It is spring. Maples have set their buds and fiddlehead ferns are about to unfurl and violets are coming up along the path leading down into the woods behind the house.

no difference to me at all

Only now, three years after he has died, does it come to me, the depth of disappointment and the truth of what I wanted him to say. To name a place, any place, not so much for his own sake but for mine, to name the place from which he came, a place of origin, of ultimate belonging, of going forth in the beginning and coming back in the end, where the fine end tips of his roots, spread out over a lifetime across the world, would always be found. *Take me back to Norway* would have been good, very good in fact. To sprinkle him in the deep waters of Hardanger, in springtime when melting snow in the mountains spawns thousands of waterfalls tumbling down into the fjord as cherry trees come into bloom.

take me home

Yes, I would have said, and gladly. I have imagined it more than once, the train from Oslo to Bergen, my father's remains resting on the seat beside me, renting a car to make my way to the ferry that would take both of us *home*. His word, not mine, or at least the word I have him say on my behalf, since it has never been home to me. *Have* him say, because he did not say it, not to me or to anyone who bothered to repeat it, did not pass on the blood secret of belonging before he died.

I also would have taken him to South Dakota, where he grew up, or to Minnesota, where he was born, or to Iowa, where his grandfather Nils Måkestad (mawk-eh-stad) changed his name to Johnson as he turned himself from a sailor into a farmer and a Norwegian into an American. But my father did not ask for that, not so much as a hint, as if it never occurred to him to even think about. No gentle but irresistible tugging at his heart, no longing to return, no sigh of tender resignation to know his children would honor a father's dying wish. Because there was no dying wish. He just kept on living until he stopped because he was old and his heart didn't work anymore and then his kidneys shutting down. The body goes until it doesn't. But a wish is something different, unless you keep it to yourself.

The only thing he asked was that we burn him up, which we have done.

I do not understand how you could be close enough to death to see it coming and hear your son ask such a question, setting up one of those unforgettable moments out of which comes a story passed down across generations—*I'll never forget the day I asked your great-grandfather where he wanted his ashes to be spread, how he looked at me for the longest time before he spoke*—how you could hear such a thing and manage only a shrug and what you said. I have seen you show more interest in a piece of lemon meringue pie than what I saw in your face that day, but you may not have known what I was really asking. Even so, I find it hard to understand. Yes, I know, *I* didn't know what I was asking either, but you were the father and fathers are supposed to know such things. You were supposed to look me in the eye as if it wasn't you at all, but some ancestral presence coming through, a voice of wisdom that surprised even you, not knowing it was there until just this moment had arrived, the singular moment of passing on—*Here is who you are, no mere extension of me, but of the same stuff that I am of, from the same place, where I am going now and where you will follow in your time. And when I am gone, you will take me there and you will know what it is.*

Something like that.

The place would have a name, by which I don't mean *heaven* or *Valhalla,* but Dubuque or Hardanger, because I am still alive and need a place where I can go and close my eyes and smell the earth and tell myself that this is who I am, where I am from, which I would know because this is where, after your long life of wandering the earth, I brought you and only because you asked.

I have put the box on the shelf behind the place where I write. I do not want to look at it just now. I do not want to think that this is all I've got to work with.

The last thing you are supposed to do, if it has not been done already in one way or another, is lift a finger and point *over there* so the rest of us will know. But to leave as if it meant nothing at all is to jump from a boat adrift in the middle of the ocean and take with you not only the compass and the rudder but also the map and then pass your hand across the sky to wipe out the stars. That's the way it feels.

I have a good mind to take you out back and dump you in the woods, but that would just be a permanent reminder of what you were supposed to tell me and did not.

Dad, I *asked*.

I will have to find something better to do with you.

My family held a memorial service at Nora's and my house in Connecticut the autumn after my father died. My sister did not want her share of the ashes and so we buried some of them at the points of the four directions at the base of an old hemlock standing by a stream running through the woods behind the house. The rest I ceremoniously sprinkled into the water, imagining his remains making their way down to the Farmington River and from there into the Connecticut and eventually to the sea and across the ocean to Norway, born along on a Viking funeral barge brimming with flowers.

The fantasy felt good enough for a while, although I knew all along that I had just made it up and what a poor substitute it was for what I really needed. Now when I go down to the stream in the morning with our old Lab, Elsie Bean, I sometimes remember the spoonfuls of ashes we deposited there, but, honestly, it does almost nothing for me to think of it. This ground has no particular meaning beyond the limits of my own life, going back just the sixteen years since we came onto the land and built the house. It is uncommonly beautiful and quiet here, and I have said how much I would like to be scattered in these woods when I have died. I don't know anymore why I said this. Now it feels like a romantic lunge toward something larger that I cannot see, much less have, and even if it's more than that, I have no illusion that it's anything like what I imagined my father might have said to me and did not.

My brother tells me that he is saving his portion of the ashes for when Geraldine, our stepmother, dies, so that we can mingle their ashes together as she has asked. I don't know where he intends to scatter them, since her answer was the same as my father's right down to the shrug. "*I* don't know," she said offhandedly, with a note of exasperation mixed in, as if put out that I expected her to know, and then just staring out into the air, which I have grown used to with the progress of her Alzheimer's and the fact that she cannot see.

That leaves my own portion. I did not understand at first my sister's aversion but may have a better sense of it now. What was she to do with it, after all? What am I?

Each morning before breakfast, I go down to my writing room and sit in meditation for a half hour. Today I place my father's ashes on the table in front of the couch where I sit. I don't know why. Perhaps I imagine he's going to say what he did not when he had the chance. I sit and stare at the box with its label and rubber band and then I'm thinking that I should be feeling something profound, but what comes over me is disappointment in myself, the sense of something lacking in a son who gazes at his father's ashes and sees only a plain brown box. The meditation timer on the table beside me softly gongs, and I close my eyes, noting the disappointment, breathing in, breathing out.

Somewhere in the middle I also note my anger that it did not occur to him that it might matter not so much where he asked to have his ashes put but that he would ask at all. That someplace is better than no place. If he had asked me to spread them along the spit by the water in Sequim, a place we often walked, I could have drawn some message from it—the importance of being anchored in a love of place, a familiar view that resonates deep inside the soul. See how I can make it up, fill in the gaps? I don't need much—a clue, a few notes in a line, and I can hum the rest. He didn't have to say that it's because he loved the view or the sound of the sea, but only enough to indicate his soul's being drawn in some earthbound direction before heading off into the ether,

breathing in, breathing out

or, *lay me down beside my mother and father*, but then he would have had to tell me where his parents, my grandparents, are buried, which

I just now realize I do not know. Somewhere in the flat landscape of the upper Midwest.

I was in Fargo, North Dakota, once and when I remarked how flat it is, so unlike New England, my host laughed and said that if the ground were as smooth as a table and you dropped a marble, it would just sit there. I don't know why I thought of that just now, something about inertia, the tendency of a thing to stay where it is unless something comes along that is powerful enough to set it in motion.

Scatter me anywhere, anywhere at all. Anywhere except nowhere, which pretty much describes the view from inside a plain brown plastic box.

I am making breakfast when it comes to me, the memory of my father saying he wanted no marker for his grave in the event that he had one. Which I take to mean there should be no way for anyone to find him, nothing to stand over or beside as they remember him, no tablet with words inscribed that might evoke a memory.

I do not understand this. He lived a happy life. He died loving his wife and children and grandchildren and great-grandchildren. And yet, *I want no marker*, going out of his way to make the point, leaving no room for whatever we might feel moved to do or have for ourselves. As if he had died alone in a far-off land or the middle of the sea.

And once again I did not think to ask why not. I did not think to ask because I felt no need for something more, as if he were only expressing a personal preference having nothing to do with me.

When my mother died thirteen years ago, she asked to have a portion of her ashes spread in her garden, being careful to spread them thinly so as not to clump and to maximize the horticultural effect. Another portion she thought it would be nice to spread nearby the graves of her parents in West Salem, Wisconsin, along with a small stone to mark the spot, which my brother's daughter did some years ago. The rest was up to us to scatter as we wished. It pleased me then to sprinkle them about the base of the hemlock down by the stream behind our house and to pour the rest into the water, as I did with my sister's portion of my father ten years later. As it turns out, being pleased isn't all it's cracked up to be.

What does it matter where a body's ashes lie? Into the question steps my busy mind to push away the nagging sense of something lost and missing in my heart. *It is just a body*, I quote my mother to myself, a pile of ashes, good for the garden or to put on an icy walk, but not much else. Ever practical, the farmer's daughter, who by the time I came along was so isolated from any sense of place or kin that I grew up barely knowing aunts or uncles or cousins, who spent her winters in Mexico and the rest of the year in her house in Massachusetts, always alone. She owned the house, but, except for the garden, she acted like a transient with no interest in settling in or leaving her mark. She left everything exactly as it was the day she moved in—the wallpaper, the ugly carpeting, the old linoleum in the kitchen and bath, the chipping paint on the woodwork. She liked to quote the Buddhists on the perils of attachment and desire and the liberation of wanting nothing, by which standard she seemed to be truly free unless you noticed how she might give something away in a moment of generosity and then years later show up to take it back. Or you knew about her losing her mother when she was just a girl and happened to get a look into the inner desolation and the broken heart and the depth of longing she carried with her to the end. Or received her advice to never complain to the neighbors lest they know what matters to you, which they might use against you later on.

My father was the son of a Lutheran minister who served the people of small towns dotting the Great Plains of Montana, Minnesota, and South Dakota at the turn of the twentieth century. My father had little to say about his father in the memoir he wrote some years before he died, but whatever is the truth of it, being the son of John Lewis Johnson was enough to turn my father permanently against religion. He had little patience for the idea of God or some reality beyond what his physical senses could detect. He was tolerant of other people inquiring into the spirit and the unknown but showed no interest in it himself. And although he was an affectionate man, at least in his later years when he seemed to have suddenly discovered the power of a hug or saying, 'I love you,' he had no emotional curiosity that I ever saw. Not once in the almost sixty years that I knew him did he ask me how I actually felt about anything. He was interested in history and politics and people, but only in collecting their outward stories—their wealth and worldly accomplishments in particular—and not their inner lives, of which he seemed strangely unaware.

All his life my father moved from place to place, from the Midwest to California to Washington, D.C., and then to Norway and Poland as an officer in the Foreign Service, to Iceland and Canada before retiring with Geraldine to the Pacific Northwest. He never lived in a house that wasn't owned and largely furnished by someone else until he was almost sixty years old. He took to his change of status with a vengeance, becoming a gardener and planting fruit trees and flowering bushes surrounded by great expanses of black plastic covered with wood chips and landscape stones, not a slip of green showing except by his design. The impression was of a tiny island conceived from the obsession with detail of someone possessed by the peculiar coupling of urgency and a surplus of time.

He installed a sprinkler system with an elaborate timer for when they were away, which turned out to be quite a lot. They spent months sailing around the world, went to Africa and Russia and up and down the Alaskan coast. They took to spending winters in Arizona in someone else's house or apartment with someone else's furniture and dishes and someone else's artwork on the walls. All the while, the interior of their own house stayed exactly the same year after year, like a museum that never goes beyond the permanent exhibit. Whatever was in a particular place on the previous visit—the picture of Iceland on the wall, the Dutch figure on the mantle, the extra toiletries in the guest bathroom—could be counted on to be there on the next.

And yet for everything staying the same, they were, inside themselves, transients to the end, vagabonds setting up camp each night with everything just so, arranging around them their collection of precious possessions like amulets against the night.

And how ironic it is that the last surviving parent should be my other-mother, Geraldine, and that her chief complaint should be that she doesn't know who or where she is. Or who I am to her.

What does it really matter where we are? My mind goes blank, unable to grasp the question. But my heart is not put off so easily.

When I was a student in college and people would ask where I was from, I used to say it was wherever I happened to be. I don't think I was trying to be evasive or coy or clever or even in-the-moment Buddhist. I simply didn't know what to say and yet had to come up with something to put them off, and this was the best that I could do.

Where are you from? Am I the only one who finds the question difficult? Beyond the social ritual of *hi how are you I'm fine blah blah where are you from?* what does it mean and where does it go? People aren't wanting to know where I was ten minutes or an hour ago, so how far back do they mean? When I went to college in New Hampshire, I came from Massachusetts, but when I lived in Massachusetts, I was from Norway, and in Norway, from Washington, and in Washington, from my mother, and in my mother . . . which is where it gets easier to be from wherever I am right now.

I don't need such ruses anymore, being grown up with fully developed social skills. When people ask where I'm from, I say what is expected without letting on that it might be untrue or less than true or other than true without being false. Not exactly.

I am from the northwest hills of Connecticut is what I tell them now. Literally true and geographically accurate, but not in my heart, in that seat of longing and loneliness and feeling lost that shows up in my dreams and drifts through my mind as I stare out the window of one more airplane taking me to and from one more speaking engagement, taking me away or returning me 'home,' suspended in the air, none of it seeming real enough to quiet the disquiet inside me.

Figuring this out—source and origin, the who or what or where that I am from—is more than a puzzle, a scientific question, and inseparable from the problem of what to do with my share of what remains of my father.

And it is a problem. I could not keep that box in the laundry room forever. In fact, the moment I took it down, I passed a point of no return, knowing that until I find a proper place for it to be, it will remain in the open, where I cannot help but see it every day. I cannot just get rid of it. And I cannot leave it for my children to come across when Nora and I are dead.

No, my father's ashes must *go* somewhere that I *intend*, must be *placed* in a way that gives meaning not just to him but to me—whatever that means—and to my family, to my brother and my sister and all our children, such that if they should ask, I could tell them and they would nod and smile, *good, I'm glad, just so.*

My father's ashes must go to what or wherever he is from, and yet I say 'what' and 'where' only for want of something better, because I don't know exactly what I mean beyond a feeling that draws me to the words—which is, after all, the problem, the lack of more to go on. And while I'm at it, I might as well add *to whom. Who what where* is my father from? And when I ask the question for him, is it not also for me?

To know the *where* includes some idea of *who*. What leaps to mind when I hear that someone's from New York or Kenya or Japan is not only geography or scenery but also varieties of human beings. People and place are inseparable, which is why a person who claims to be from nowhere is so mysterious in a disturbing and even frightening sort of way. I cannot know who you really are without knowing who and where you are from.

This should be easy. My father came from Norwegians who lived in Norway, on his father's side from Hardanger and on his mother's from somewhere north of Oslo. I know this from an old book written in Norwegian that shows a portion of my father's lineage going all the way back to the fourteenth century. And if that isn't good enough, there is this: several years before he died, I asked my father if he thought of himself as a Norwegian—*a* Norwegian—and he said *oh yes* but then was quick to add that, of course, he was also American. I asked him what it was about being Norwegian that meant so much to him, and he glowed as he spoke of the people and the culture and the land. But when I asked him if he thought of being American in the same way, he did not hesitate to say *no*, it was not the same at all.

That would seem to mean that somewhere in Norway is where his ashes ought to go, except that he made no mention of it when I asked, this man who grew up speaking four dialects of Norwegian.

And he was so careful to reassure me that he was American, as if worried that I might think badly of him if he did not. But why would he worry about that, a white man whose ancestors came here generations ago, who spoke English with no discernible accent, who served in the U.S. Navy during World War II followed by a career as a diplomat with letters of appointment signed by the president of the United States? In spite of this, was he telling me that his love of Norway and his sense of himself as Norwegian exposed him to an accusation of disloyalty that he felt a need to defend himself against? Was the appearance of indifference a ruse to cover up ambivalence? Was he actually afraid to let it be known that he wanted nothing more than to be scattered across the deep waters of Hardangerfjord below the village of Måkestad whose very name—*home of the seagulls*—his grandfather had abandoned in order to become American?

Perhaps 'ruse' is putting it too strongly. He may not have been consciously false to me. It would not surprise me if his longing and fear were buried so deep that even he did not know how much his answer to my question mattered after all.

Then again, after decades of living all over the world, my father may have ended his life as a man without a place, a displaced person for whom the price of being able to fit in anywhere was to wind up being from nowhere, routinely singing the praises of whatever country he was posted to, the diplomatic version of loving the one you're with if you can't be with the one you love.

Or to be from wherever you happen to be.

The better you get at this way of being in the world, the more likely you are to forget what and where it was you loved in the first place, or how much, how irresistibly, right down to the end, drawing you back, everything else falling away for what it was, a temporary distraction, a wandering detour off the path that always leads you home.

I will never know the truth of what went on inside him unless, perhaps, he comes to me in a dream. And there is still the problem of not knowing where *I* want him to be. I am not indifferent or ambivalent to that, because I am still here, and what becomes of me is yet to come.

Almost twenty years ago, when Nora and I were building the house we live in now, in the foothills of the Berkshires in the northwest corner of Connecticut, I would drive down Route 44 going west from Hartford and then turn onto a road running north through a gently sloping valley. The moment I turned the wheel in that direction I could feel a sinking down inside myself, as if I'd been holding my breath in anticipation of a long wait being over at last. The road winds past houses and then through Canton Center with its old general store—a historic landmark—with a tiny post office on one side and a Congregational Church on the other, whose tall white spire from a vantage point farther off would poke through the trees in one of those sure signs of being somewhere in New England. Across the street from the church is a small one-story wood-frame building that used to be an extension of the town library. A hundred yards farther on, as you turn left onto Barbourtown Road, only a few miles from our house, is the elementary school and then the fieldstone house of Peg Perry—who has since died, the town's cantankerous, chain-smoking librarian who was also sister to Katharine Hepburn—and then the Perry farm, the dairy cows grazing in the field close by the road as I drive by.

I do love this place, *our little piece of heaven* I like to call it, with its woods and hills and quiet stillness and white-tailed deer and red foxes and black bears. I love coming home to it, to see the ridgeline of the hills along the valley rise out of the trees. And to judge from the tears coming into my eyes, it touches something more than a simple love for what I have, but also a sadness and a longing this place has the power to evoke but not assuage. I wish I was *from* this place, I *should have* been from here or someplace like it, or from Norway, *I should have been Norwegian*, the words sounding in my mind, awkward, ridiculous, and strange.

Sometimes when I've had enough of the news and imagine myself living somewhere else, a country whose government makes me feel less frightened or ashamed, I think of Norway, of Oslo in particular, where we lived for two years when I was a boy. I imagine living there now, an aging ex-patriot writer finding a more appreciative audience. But the fantasy dissolves as quickly as I can do the math, Norway being the most expensive place to live on the planet, because the government, true to its socialist tendencies, shares the wealth from its North Sea oil with all its citizens and not just a wealthy few. And then there is my not speaking Norwegian and the fact that I would be utterly alone, knowing no one except a few relatives in Bergen, and that not one iota of my longing would find release in that place where the only thing that truly belongs is my longing for it.

When people ask me now where I'm from, I name the place where I live, which is technically correct but not quite true to the question that I often hear in my mind. Because to live in a place and to be from a place are not the same. When I was younger, I didn't mind living out the difference. I was restless and preoccupied with family and work and figuring out what I could have and what I could not, and so being from nowhere didn't seem to matter. But now it does, because I am getting older and my parents are dead and my mind is more available to such things as death and regret and the nature and meaning of a life. And, of course, there is the little brown box.

Opening my eyes from meditation this morning, I look out the window of my writing room at the rain, avoiding the box on the table, small and mute.

Beside me is a stack of black-and-white photographs from my father's life. On top is one of him as a boy, dated August 8, 1915, when he was three years old and living where he was born, in Wells, Minnesota. He is sitting outside by a wire fence, on a little chair that looks like a grownup chair sized to fit a child. Behind him are trees and a neighbor's house beneath a milky sky. He is dressed in striped overalls and a white shirt with a scarf around his neck and a broad-brimmed bowl of a hat above a grin. He is holding what looks like a potato, and beside him on the grass is a bowl. His feet are on the ground and he looks happy. On the white space that borders the image is written 'Valde,' the childhood nickname for Valdemar Nels Luther Johnson, the 'Nels' a variation on his grandfather's name and 'Luther' for the founder of the faith that his father, my grandfather, was called to preach. I don't know where the 'Valdemar' came from, except for the slew of Valdemars who ruled Sweden or Denmark at one time or another—Valdemar the Great, Valdemar the Victorious, Prince Valdemar. Maybe that or maybe my grandparents just liked the sound of it.

Other pictures in a similar vein may have been taken on the same day, judging from the sky and the season and his clothes. In one of my favorites he is up in a tree with his Aunt Emma, who is wearing a white dress, which makes me wish I had known such an aunt who would climb a tree with a little boy. Another shows the house with its white-railed porch running along the front, flowers, bushes, trees and shade, a winding walkway made of stone. There are images of grand-parents from both sides of the family, his mother's parents—Olsens—

looking stern near the end of a hard life. There are none of his father's mother, but there are two photos of Nils, his paternal grandfather. In the first, he is nearing middle age, with a trimmed beard and a steady, soulful look in his eyes. In the other, he is an old man on the near side of ninety, standing in the backyard, dressed in a dark suit, his face covered by a full beard extending down his chest, a glint of pleasure in his eyes as he holds the handles of a wheelbarrow in which sit my father and his brother, Erling. The date is July 1917, toward the end of World War I, and my father is five years old. Behind them are rocking chairs in the shade beneath the trees.

There is one interior scene of the living room in Wells, sunlight coming through a window on the left by the upright piano against the wall. On the reverse side of the photo is a note signed, *Love Daddy and Mother*, explaining the scene to my father, who was only six when the family moved away. In a photo of South Dakota taken in 1924 when my father was twelve, he is kneeling on the ground with another boy, a barn in the background, few trees to soften the flat, dry landscape. A dog is between them, all three smiling as they squint into the sun.

I remember what my father said after reading a collection of short stories set in Montana, which he likened to South Dakota, that he liked the stories well enough, but their sense of place gave him no pleasure. He felt none of the beauty that the author drew, shaking his head as he looked away. There was a finality to that gesture, like the soft closing of a door so as not to wake someone sleeping on the other side, that surprised me then and makes me wonder now, the feelings strong and implacable and, for him, inexpressible. Had I asked, I expect he would have said something about there being no mountains or forest or body of water so large you couldn't see the other side. He might have said something about how hard it was to be the minister's son in a small town. But I doubt he would have offered anything more, held close in the silence as he looked away.

I wake up to news of the kind of bloody struggle that seems always to be going on somewhere in the world. The story is from Africa, but it could have been Ireland or Iraq or the West Bank or Bosnia. And those are just the places that come readily to mind so early in the morning. The pattern is numbingly the same—killing and rape and starvation and so much hatred, grief piled upon grief, and you have to wonder how anyone can stand it.

In Bosnia it was called *ethnic cleansing*, ethnicity inseparable from geography. Wouldn't it be so much simpler if they could be more like my father, one place no better than another?

I try to imagine telling that to Israeli settlers watching their house being torn down or a Palestinian living in a refugee camp, the look of disbelief on their faces at the idea of giving up their relation to land that to them lies at the heart of their existence, to be displaced, to suffer a kind of death, a form of nonexistence, the Diaspora, the coming apart in the scattering of seed away from the land to which it is indigenous.

At least that is how I imagine it from a distance, because I have never felt that way myself, because I am not indigenous to anywhere, not what you would call 'aboriginal' or 'native,' qualities I grew up equating with primitive and savage, uncivilized and invariably 'dark.' So it comes easily, this feeling that those who go on fighting and hating over land must somehow be inferior to those who can rise above such things, cut loose from crude attachments to ethnicity and place to roam the earth and claim and settle land that is home to someone else.

Immigrants do well to have the gift of mimicry. My father had such a gift and it suited him to the diplomatic corps, where he was expected to be the face of the government of the United States, to give voice to policies whether he believed in them or not. He was fluent in Russian and Polish in addition to Norwegian and English, so you couldn't tell where he was really from if he did not want you to know.

When I was in college in the late 1960s, I visited my father in Minneapolis, where he was a guest lecturer in political science at the University of Minnesota. The Vietnam War was going strong, and he spoke of students challenging him at presentations on U.S. foreign policy. I couldn't be sure whether he was bragging or asking for sympathy, whether he was angry with them or angry that his job required him to make himself a public target as a surrogate for the government. I also couldn't tell whether he was against the war or not or even both at once.

Many years later I wrote a novel, *Nothing Left to Lose*, a story of a family in crisis during the Vietnam War, in which the father, an emotionally damaged veteran of World War II, keeps the trauma to himself, even from his wife, but especially from his sons. Not knowing the truth of what they're getting into, the boys volunteer to fight, and when the first son is reported missing in combat, the fabric of silence and denial and betrayal that has held the family together begins to come apart.

My father, then in his eighties, read the novel and called me up.

"I'm sorry," he said, and I thought, *what a strange thing for him to say after reading one of my books*, and when I asked him why, he said it was because he had never said anything to me about the war, back when I was young and having to deal with it as all young men had to do in one way or another. "I didn't know," he said. "If I had known, I would have said something."

It was the only time he said he was sorry to me for anything. I don't remember what I said, I was so startled to hear this coming from my father. Startled that my novel had moved him so, but even more that he had seen himself and me in the story, which I had not—consciously at least—while writing it.

So my father was against the war. Except when he was not.

And it did not matter where his ashes would be spread, made no difference to him at all.

A light rain in the air outside my window, the woods leafing in. Yesterday, in a bookstore, walking by a display of maps, I stopped in front of Iowa and beside it, Minnesota. South Dakota was tucked in behind Kentucky.

I buy all three without knowing exactly why beyond a vague notion to spread them out and sit with them awhile without anyone hovering over me to make sure I don't damage the merchandise. After all, what if I can't fold them up again, which often happens with maps—that to find your way, you have to open something that you won't be able to put back the way you found it.

I open the map of Iowa on the table beside me. A great expanse of white, crisscrossed with colored lines, splotches of yellow to mark the cities—Des Moines, Waterloo, Cedar Rapids, Iowa City, Davenport—thin blue lines for rivers. Most striking is what appears as empty space, so far between one place and another, land where no one lives. And all the roads intersecting at right angles to make a gridlike geometry of neatly laid out farms and fields.

It takes a while to locate the village of Thor, where my great-grandparents became farmers and where my cousins Loretta and Jim—whom I've never heard of until a few days ago—now live. Thor is halfway between rivers marked Boone and Des Moines. An inch or so to the south is the larger town of Fort Dodge and next to that a finely worded notation in red pointing to the *Fort Mus. & Frontier Vil.* I scan the map for Indian reservations, but they are well hidden if they exist at all, although plenty of Native names are attached to places—Ottumwa, Oskaloosa, Pocahontas, Cherokee, Ottawattamie, Keokuk, Sioux.

In the top right corner is a bit of Minnesota and enough of Wisconsin to show La Crosse, a few miles from West Salem, where my mother was born.

I align the maps edge to edge, the roads connecting one to another, and find myself wondering how long it would take to cover the distance.

I find an aerial view of the upper Midwest on the Internet. It is hard not to notice how green it is across Iowa and Minnesota and eastern South Dakota and how desolate and brown the land becomes farther west and north, where the reservations are concentrated.

I stare out the window at the rain, coming down harder now, and the wind moving through the trees.

On a shelf beside my writing table is a picture of my grandmother, who died of cancer at the age of thirty-six and left my mother without a mother of her own. She is sitting in a chair, her elbow leaning lightly on the arm, her beautiful, intelligent face turned as she gazes to the side. I never met her, which is why I have her there where I can see her. Her face opens up a longing in me to know what is going on behind her eyes, the sound of her voice when she would have spoken to me, the words she would have used, tender and protective as she took my hand.

But this picture was taken just a year or two before she died, far short of being old enough to be my grandmother, so in a way I am looking not at my grandmother but at my mother's mother, which is not the same. But I can imagine whatever I want, which is all I will ever have of her.

How calmly she is absorbed in gazing away from the camera, thinking of me, I imagine. I look at her for a long time, the silence in the room coming in around us until suddenly I sense the slightest shaking of her head and then the movement of a sigh, which is when she would have said my name and asked me to come closer, beckoning with her hand.

And then it comes over me that I have never seen the place where she is buried, or my grandfather, or anyone, for that matter, who is kin to me. I have never stood on the ground and looked down at the marker and the letters that make a name that is also my own. Those places out on the Plains are no more real to me than the lines and notations on the maps spread out on the floor. And just above, on the table, is the little box with what remains of my father.

Edward R. Murrow once remarked that it takes a while to see the obscure. The obvious, he said, takes longer.

My father cannot stay here, which means I will have to take his ashes and get on a plane and go either east or west.

To the east is Norway, but whenever I think of leaving him there, such a feeling of sadness and loss comes over me that it seems impossible.

So, then, it will have to be west.

The decision to go releases the energy I've been holding since I took the box down from the shelf in the laundry room.

I will be on my own on the Great Plains in places I have never seen, not through my own eyes, on my own terms. I will rent a car and go wherever I want, at my own pace, seeing what I want to see. And I will have what I imagine will be my own private communion with a past and a history and, most important, a lineage that has so far been invisible to me.

I feel the excitement of moving toward something new, and in a burst of activity I manage to submerge the sense of unease that has been following me around for days. I shake it off as I weave the planning of the trip into the rhythm of my day. I will go to Iowa and Minnesota and South Dakota, to Thor and Wells and Hayti, the three points of the triangle that launched my father into the life that helped give birth to me. I look up phone numbers for town and county offices that hold land records that will show where my ancestors made their homes. I locate Lutheran churches where my grandfather may have preached. I look up libraries and historical museums. I find histories and begin to read. I make phone calls.

I am most interested in the farm in Thor, a town consisting of a handful of streets crossing at right angles, barely widening the road, a mouse swallowed by a snake. The woman who answers the phone in the county auditor's office says she has records going back to 1850 and that I should come on over and have a look. When I tell her that my great-grandfather gave up the sea to become a farmer, she says, "Oh, one of those," and I think, *he was a type*, a 'one of those,' part of a great stream of humanity flowing west, women and men leaving everything behind to take up something new, to be changed by the land into someone they had not known they could ever be.

At first, the assistant in the Lutheran church in Wells cannot find a trace of my grandfather's having preached there at all. When I hang up the phone, I am wondering if we could possibly have gotten it wrong, my father not born in Wells after all, and the wondering makes him somehow less substantial in my mind, less real, harder to hold on to as my father, shaking the roots of my connection.

She calls back a few days later, and I am relieved to hear that she has found him in an old book, J. L. Johnson, who was pastor there from 1903 to 1918.

In Hayti, they find the record right away, 1918 to 1934, with no mention of where he went from there.

I am a detective sniffing out a trail, uncovering clues. I make diagrams with names and dates, connecting people and places with arrows and question marks. Martha, a librarian in Humboldt, Iowa, offers to photocopy pages from the early history of settlement there and mail them out to me.

I telephone my cousin Bill who lives near Minneapolis, the son of my father's brother, Erling. We have a long talk. It is the first time in my life that I am having an extended conversation with a cousin. It is hard to believe when it comes to me, hanging up the phone, that such a thing could be, and yet here it is. My mind is astonished while my heart is more subdued, a sadness over the long and lonely silence that has ended only now.

Before I call him, I make the skeleton of a genealogy with mostly blank space, and as he speaks into the phone I am writing furiously, there being so much that I never knew—that my great-grandmother was Margrete Ullensvang, whose last name is the name of the district in Norway where she was born, which was also the point of origin for Nils, although on the other side of the fjord; that my grandmother was Josephine Olsen, and that it was her sister Emma up in the tree with my father in the photograph; that I have relations in Thor who lived on my great-grandparents' farm until selling it just 2 years ago, ending 126 years of that land's being in our family. *Our* family.

My desk is covered with notes and diagrams, phone numbers and maps. One day I find myself staring at the calendar, wondering when I will do this thing. The weather will be good at the end of May, early June. Over the next few days, I sketch out in my mind how much time I will need in one place or another. At first I think to go chronologically, starting in Thor and ending in South Dakota, but that would mean a five-hour drive coming back to Minneapolis to catch my plane home. It would make more sense to do it the other way around, going backward in time.

I count up the days, nine in all, not counting travel. So, it seems, I have a plan.

Weeks go by. I have yet to make an airline reservation or rent a car or telephone a single hotel. I go into my office, and the first thing I see are the slips of paper all over my desk, nagging me to set myself in motion. I do my work and go away, unmoved.

And then one day I wake and look out the window at the light infusing the eastern sky, and it comes to me that I am afraid.

Afraid that nothing will happen, that I will carry my father's ashes all that way only to bring them back again because I will not find the place where they belong. Or, worse, that I will discover that no such place exists.

It helps to say it aloud. I practice on Nora. I don't want to go yet I have to go, and she nods in recognition of the ambivalence and fear she sees in my face, hears in my voice.

The more I say the words, the smaller they become. I do not want to go. I have to go.

The moment I buy the ticket, I feel something let go inside me and I think it will be easy now, but then days go by before I remind myself that I'll also need a car, and it's a few days more before I go online to shop around, and even then nothing comes of it.

Getting me to do these simple things is turning out to be like trying to coax a frightened animal out of its hole. I would get on myself about it, except I also know that fear is never stupid. It always has a reason.

There is the experience of living in the world without a sense of having a place of origin where I truly belong and am from in a deep and elemental way. I am discovering that I can live this without allowing myself to know it, especially when I consider what an awful feeling it can be. There are ways to distract myself—in work, in buying what I can have or longing for what I can't, in worrying about the details, in chasing the job, in reaching for the bigger hit, the higher high, the rung that I can see, the pursuit of happiness, even if I don't know exactly what it is, telling myself that we're the best, the exceptional Americans, who don't have to bother with such things, with origins and belonging. Keep on the move, like a nomad pretending to be from wherever I happen to be and telling myself that even if I'm not, it doesn't matter anyway.

So, where are you from?

Well, if you mean where I was born—

And there it is, the 'well' tossed off even though it is the pivot on which everything turns, as in, *well, I don't actually know what you mean, but let's try this. . . .*

A person can live a life that way. I have in one way or another, although I like to think not all the time. I write, I meditate, I talk it out, I try to be conscious and stay in the moment, the here and the now, all of that, and to some extent I do. Except when I do not, the astronaut untethered from the mother ship and floating off into space, waving his arms like a child in a snowsuit, his body slowly spinning round.

I am afraid of losing my illusions. I am afraid of what may be true that I haven't allowed myself to know, and that if I actually go into the world and cannot find a place for my father's ashes and must bring them back with me, then I will know, in a way I will not forget, just who I am, a man from nowhere. At least that is what frightens me, and not to go is never to find out one way or another.

Except that now I know too much and have a nonrefundable plane ticket.

Today I rent a car. The hotels I can do tomorrow.

The playwright Lillian Hellman wrote a memoir called *Pentimento* after the practice of layering one painted image on top of another on the same canvas. It might be due to a mistake or an artist's change of mind or the need to reuse the canvas. Or perhaps not wanting to look at the image anymore, wanting to forget what it reminds them of. It comes from the Latin term meaning to regret and to repent.

I think of it now because Dee Brown's book *Bury My Heart at Wounded Knee* came into my thoughts a few days ago, and ever since I've been unable to get it out. When I first took my father's ashes off the shelf, I thought this was just between him and me. But then it is also about my ancestors in this country and who they were and the land on which they lived and died, some piece of which I am hoping will be the place where my father belongs. Deeper still is the story of Native Americans displaced and dispossessed, and a depth of horror and sorrow and loss and grief such as I have never had to know.

And I am kept from knowing by a buffer of obliviousness that is so subtle that I rarely get a glimpse of it. One of those moments was several years ago, when I spoke at the White Privilege Conference in Pella, Iowa. I told the story of my mother's grandparents, Henry Dudley and Jenny Griswold Dudley, and their dairy farm in western Wisconsin and how their prosperity was tied to the institution of slavery in the South even though they lived in the North and owned no slaves themselves. I described how for hundreds of years, the combination of cotton, sugar, and rum produced a wealthy industrializing society with a huge appetite for food, which farmers did well to provide. I went on to tell how their modest portion of the national prosperity made possible by slavery was passed down across generations of my family to the present day. I wanted to show that the institution of slavery not only is in the past but is also current and material and involves us all.

When I was done, the audience gave its applause, and I left the platform and found an empty chair in the crowd, content that I had done what I came to do as well as I knew how.

A little while later, I didn't see it coming when another speaker pointed out that my great-grandparents' farm was on land that had been taken from Native Americans. There was something in the way the audience roared its approval that left me sitting there trying to contain my embarrassment over what felt like a public rebuke.

When I got over that, I could consider how easy it was to not notice how deeply the history of this country is embedded in my life.

Since that day in Pella, when I speak on race I always mention the history of the Ho Chunk tribe on whose land my great-grandparents built their farm. Even so, it was some years after Pella that it dawned on me that the land that Nora and I are living on now has a similar history, taken from Native Americans who did not want to give it up. I didn't know the name of the tribe or who they were or what became of them, so I looked it up. The Massacoe, who, as far as I could tell, no longer exist.

I look at my maps of Iowa, Minnesota, and South Dakota, land soaked in blood spilled in taking it away from Peoples who had lived on it for thousands of years and wanted only to go on as before. I have not been searching for that history, which came up briefly and almost by accident. I have been looking for a link between myself and what I imagine to be the land of my ancestors, the People of my origin. Wanting to imagine. Needing to.

Dee Brown writes that "the Indians knew that life was equated with the earth," which I think means you cannot understand a life without knowing the land it came from and where it was lived, because the two are one and the same. But I grew up in a society that looks upon land as a temporary place to live, to set up shop, a resource to be seized and controlled and exploited, ruined, if need be, in the pursuit of wealth and power. The last thing that would occur to us is to look upon the land and see ourselves, or to look deep into our own eyes, our faces, the lines that etch our lives upon our bodies, and see the land.

I am a white man, born and raised, the land therefore a mystery to me, making me a mystery to myself. And if Native People are right about the land, then it is not a sort of mystery to be solved like an engineering problem but instead something that can be known only through the body, and for that the body must be on the land.

What I know about my ancestors and the land has come mostly through books, without the urgency that I am feeling now in these days before I set out on this journey in the middle of my sixty-third year, in a way I never would have imagined, through the body of my father.

This feeling of not wanting to go, the fear, coalesces in a knot that wakes me in the morning while the eastern sky is still dark. I lie in bed and look out the window as Nora sleeps beside me. Elsie Bean comes over for a scratch, goes back to bed. I stare at the trees outlined against the sky and think to myself that I don't know what I'm doing or where I'm going even though I have a plane ticket, a car, places to stay, names and numbers of people who know my name. I have studied maps and know pretty well how to get from one place to another and some idea of how long it will take. But all the preparation is an empty shell, and I do not know what I am supposed to find to fill it in, what it is supposed to *be* when I am done with it. Who I'm supposed to be.

When Nils Måkestad came to the United States, he was just twenty-five years old and completely on his own, having abandoned his career in the Norwegian merchant marine by jumping ship in Halifax, Nova Scotia. I imagine there was no one to receive him, to take him in, to sympathize, comfort, or commiserate, to give advice or point him on his way. He had to figure it all out by himself with what he had, including little money and even less English, which may explain why he stopped in Chicago to go back to sailing for a while, this time on the Great Lakes. He worked at this for seven more years and then, for some reason lost to us, finally gave up the water for the land and went to Lee County, Illinois, due west of Chicago and three hundred miles southeast of Thor. I don't know what he did while he was there, but he stayed for just a year before joining the massive westward movement of white people to settle land advertised as 'empty' and there for the taking. By then, he may have been part of a group of Norwegian immigrants, which I gather from the number of people listed in the history of Thor who all came there in the same year, 1872.

It says that he married Margaret Larson in February and they arrived in Thor that spring. I pause over her being named Larson instead of Ullensvang, the name Bill had given to me. They grew up on opposite sides of Hardangerfjord and did not know each other despite the short distance between them across the water. So, at last they were not alone, and together they would create a farm of 320 acres and raise five children, including my grandfather John Lewis.

I can only assume that Nils, who had by then changed his name to Johnson, must have been well acquainted with fear, especially in those early years, out there in the middle of a new land that was so unlike what he and Margaret knew at home, unable to understand what was said to them or to make themselves understood, not to mention the insecurities of a farmer's life. And then there were the Native Americans, whom they would call 'Indians' and against whom, in the 1870s, the United States was in a state of war all over the western Plains, a war that would not be done until the murder of Sitting Bull followed by the massacre at Wounded Knee, South Dakota, in 1890, when my grandfather was twelve years old.

Everyone must have been afraid, especially Native People watching the white flood tide coming on, inexorable, unstoppable, driven by a murderous hunger for land and buffalo hides and lumber and gold.

By the time my great-grandparents arrived in Thor, the front lines of that war had moved farther west, but it was not so far away in place or time not to have figured in how they saw themselves in the world.

And so it makes sense that my own journey into this history should bring up the fear that has dogged me almost from the start, a sense of being unprotected, ill-equipped, alone. It is, in part, a personal fear born out of my own life, and yet it also appears to me as something older passed on across generations, a collective fear lodged in a collective memory of the history of race in America. I watch a black man strive to become president and cannot help but see the fear swirling all around him, lodged in a desperate desire to have this campaign not be about race, to not remind us of race, to let us go on telling the story of this nation and our ancestors and ourselves and not have it be about race.

I write books, I give speeches, I run workshops to help people come to grips with this fear, but while I am writing or standing in front of an audience, I am not myself afraid, not of them or of what I've come to say. Until now, when the problem of my father's ashes makes the subject of race about me in a way it never was before. Now it is about my ancestors, my portal into this land, the anchor of my sense of belonging and rootedness. I know that what is going on in this country *is* about race and in one way or another has always *been* about race, but at the same time, I feel that part of myself that joins in wishing it weren't so. I may know too much to go past wishing to believing, but in the silence of my own denial, when I am simply going about my life as a white man in a white man's country, my true state of mind is something closer to belief.

I look at the words on the screen, aware that just now I referred to myself as a white man, which is not remarkable, being something I do routinely in my line of work. But this morning it feels different, has greater weight, because it is about me in a way that it was not before.

It is strange that I do not see myself as a New Englander. I have lived here most of my life, and three different lines of my mother's ancestry—Dudleys, Baileys, and Griswolds—first settled here more than three hundred years ago. I would rather live here than anywhere else, for the architecture of older homes and public buildings, the shape of the land, the wooded hills and valleys, the seasons. But if I had to move away from here, I wouldn't feel the loss of something that defines who I am. New England is the place where I live and I like it very much, but it isn't where I'm from or where I must return.

Then again, maybe it's not so strange after all. I was born in Washington, D.C., and by the time we came to New England, I was eight years old and had lived in Norway for two years as a foreigner who had to adapt to someone else's language and culture. If I wanted to play with children in the neighborhood where we lived, I had to learn Norwegian because they spoke little English. And so I did.

I brought back with me from Norway a sense of a world larger than the United States and full of people perfectly happy to be where they are and with no desire to give it up to live in the United States, much less become American. It was a good thing to have a larger view so early on, but it also meant beginning my life as a displaced person. I was cut loose from roots that would limit me to a single, narrow point of view, but I also lacked that very thing, an essential rootedness in place.

We settled in Andover, Massachusetts, and I worked at getting used to feeling odd, the only one in my school who had lived abroad, whose father now was not living with us at home. Oddness can be a badge of distinction but also a lonely and disaffecting thing. Maybe that's all this is, what my father's ashes have opened up in me, my own peculiar story.

And yet, there is also this. Except for Native Americans, this is a nation of people whose ancestors, if not they themselves, gave up their native places in coming here, or, in the case of enslaved Africans, were kidnapped and forced to give it up, all knowing they most likely would never go back again, would never know who they were in the way that only indigenous beings can know in the land they are truly from. This story is the human ground on which everything else was built in the making of this country, and regardless of what people have done to make themselves and their descendants 'American,' it is still this that we are standing on, that runs in our blood and inhabits our dreams. Everyone here came from somewhere else and we try to make that bearable by sharing in the illusion that all it takes is the passage of time, generation after generation, to erase that fact from our memories or to make it appear so small and obscure that it doesn't matter anymore.

And then a voice in my mind chimes in to say that it doesn't matter because if you go back far enough, even Native Americans came from somewhere else, or so the scientists tell us. So isn't it just a question of time before we, the latest newcomers, become native to this land, if we are not already?

The logic of it might be enough if logic were all this is about, but it's not. When my father looked away and shrugged and said it made no difference, he was conveying something that he himself may not have known, something passed to him before I was born and without anyone being aware of it. A question, a doubt, an existential gap, a hole a person could fall through and not stop falling. Whatever it is, he passed it on to me, and now it points down a path I will have to follow as long as the ashes are in my keeping, until I find the place where they belong, which, it occurs to me, may be the point, what ashes are really for, the reason a body is so hard to reduce to nothing.

In these days before I leave for Minnesota, there are phone calls still to make, road maps to print out, but mostly nothing left to do but pack and go. I am suspended between one place and another, my body in motion, but my heart holding still.

I am trying not to think about what will happen. I tell myself I am living in uncertainty and should just get used to it, the whole point being to find out what happens next, all good advice, full of Buddhist acceptance and letting go, but still I am restless to fill in the emptiness, which is what I'm most afraid of, not of something bad, but of nothing at all.

I spend my days working my way through a pile of library books about Native Americans and the things that were done to turn them into a displaced, dispossessed People. History is about the land, and if I am to find a place to receive my father, the land will tell me where that is, and I will have to know how to listen to the stories of what was lived and done upon the land, because the stories have as much to do with where I am as any coordinates on a map.

One after another, I devour books to inscribe on my heart an inner map, a hedge against winding up someplace where I don't know where I am or how to read the signs and am unable to find my way home again. Or a place where I don't belong, where I am trespassing, even though the land is occupied by white people just like me, some of whom are my relations. It is not enough to make me safe, not in my heart.

I read and then play the piano and look at photographs.

I read some more.

The Great Chicago Fire was in 1871. I go on, then stop, my mind trolling until I remember that my great-grandfather left Chicago in that year. Was he there for the Great Fire? Would he have stayed were it not for Mrs. O'Leary's cow? And if he had, what would have become of marrying and farming and children and all the rest, including me?

The history of what happened on the land and the history of my family are converging in my mind, and somewhere inside those stories there is me.

It is Sunday of Memorial Day weekend, and my plane leaves tomorrow. In Minneapolis, I'll have lunch with my cousins Jim and Bill, sons of my father's older brother, Erling. Since I e-mailed them about my trip, they have been generous and kind, Jim even inviting me to spend my last night at his house in St. Paul, where we meet tomorrow.

Why am I surprised? Why the impulse to say no? Shyness? Embarrassed at being sixty-two years old and knowing so little about my own family? Or the fear that if I allow myself to feel what I have been without for my entire life, it will crack me in two.

I bumble through the day, not knowing what to do with myself after the hour or so that it takes to pack, already in motion and still right here. I do not want to go. I cannot wait to be off. I am standing at the edge of a high diving board, both wanting and afraid to do the very thing I have climbed all this way to do.

There is always a moment when an airplane first lifts its nose into the air and the ground falls away, when I close my eyes and say good-bye. Sometimes my eyes begin to fill, and I look down and hood my face with my hand, feigning sleep, so nobody will see. The engines strain and vibrate against the pull of the earth as we bank into a long ascending westward turn. I picture my father's ashes in my suitcase in the cargo bay down below my feet. I press my sleeve into my eyes. Here we go.

I close my eyes and think of sitting up with my father the night before he died, talking and singing to him even though he was unconscious. We were together in a way that we had never been before, stripped down to the fact of his living and his dying, each breath until the last, the feel of him beneath my fingers as I stoked his face and hair, the sound of my voice in the room, the murmurs that came from him when I withdrew my hand, *no, no, don't stop*. In my whole life, he never asked me for anything, never came to me in need, until that night, or so it seemed, and brought forth such a tenderness between us, simple and real, filling the room. Nothing else mattered but that moment and then the next and the fact that he would die and I would be there with him until it was done and he was gone. At least that's what I thought, but now here we are again more than two years later, and what remains of him is packed with my belongings, toiletries, underwear, and socks.

I take out my journal and write, *Let yourself dissolve and you will know who you are,* which Nora said to me last night, no resistance, letting go, not trying to figure out. I wonder if I can, if it is possible.

The woman next to me can read what I am writing if she turns her head, but I do not care, being invisible as ghosts, my father and I. I am not really here in the sense that I imagine she is here, staring down at the book in her lap. I am in flight over the earth with the ashes of my father, everything falling away, everyone and everything I ever knew, except this movement through time and space.

I watch people getting up to move about the cabin. The flight attendant begins her slow promenade up the aisle with coffee and Diet Coke and snacks for sale. The woman next to me turns a page, and the man by the window stares into the screen of his computer. Across the way, a woman gazes out the window at clouds against the sky, while another leans down to whisper to her child, and a man in first class stretches his arms above his head and then leans back his seat to go to sleep, all of it seeming strangely removed, unless I am the one who is both strange and removed.

I think of my father's voice when he said it did not matter to him what I did with his ashes, and I wonder if he was handing me the task of coming to understand how it might matter to me.

It is a short drive from the airport to Jim's house. When I visited my father here in the 1960s, he took me on a trip to places where my relatives had lived. Our first stop was West Salem, where I saw the farmhouse where my mother grew up, and then back into Minnesota to Wells, where he was born. I have no specific memory of it, just that we were there, and a mental image of a dull and empty flatness of land against a highway overpass that I take to have been in Iowa. I don't know what time of year it was, perhaps winter, Christmas break, which might explain the lack of color and a feeling of desolation. I'm pretty sure we didn't go as far as South Dakota.

My mother's farm is gone, the farmhouse with the barn out back and the corn crib with its tin roof, where my mother and her sisters slept out in the summertime, fields and shade trees, the daylight alive with the sounds of living things, the night air still and quiet. A small shopping center is on the land where the Griswold Guernseys once grazed and produced their enviable milk and cream. I still have a half-pint glass bottle from the dairy, the words "Griswold's Guernsey milk" and "absolutely the best" in raised relief on the front. I have it only because my mother saw fit to hang on to a pair of them for almost eighty years.

There is now a parking lot where the road went by the house, where my mother's younger sister Marjorie, whom I have seen in a family photograph from the time, was struck down and killed by what was then one of the few cars in the town.

Nearby stands the small cemetery where Marjorie and other members of my mother's family are buried.

I have not been back to West Salem since my father and I were there. Over the last few weeks, I have had this feeling that I should go to West Salem, even though this trip seems to be just about my father. I should go if only to see my mother's family graves—grandparents and great-grandparents, aunts and uncles. But what will it mean to stand before the graves near manicured lawns and shopping malls? What can it possibly mean? Where would I be then but in a land of pavement and concrete and special programs to coax children to go outside because they don't want to be where there isn't an electrical outlet.

Nowhere is where.

The feeling coming up in me reminds me of when I was the stage manager in our community theater and would visit the space a few days after the closing of a show. Alone in the room full of stillness beneath the quiet, the stage empty, the set struck the morning after closing night, I would feel how the reality, the story we had created and lived with so much work and love was gone, the space hollow and emptied out, eerie, as if we were never there.

I won't go back. It feels like a dispossession, and I don't want to find out how complete it really is. I am afraid it would be too much like they were never there at all.

Jim looks like his father, thin and sharply featured. He hugs me at the door, and then there's Bill, rounder, more like his mother, holding out his hand, and then I see a woman friend of Jim's as well, perhaps invited as a kind of buffer to make it easier after so many years, leavening the dough. We sit around the table in the large open kitchen, and there is pot roast and potatoes and salad and dessert and lively conversation, and when they ask me why I've come, I say that after my father died I thought it time to visit places I had heard of but never been, which is a truth that makes easier the lie of not saying what's in my suitcase in the car.

I do not tell them, because I don't want to come back and have to say I couldn't find a place for him and then have to explain about listening to the land, which I don't even understand now, and then see the looks on their faces. I do not tell them because they may want to know what Native Americans have got to do with burying my father, and I won't know what to say because I won't have an answer, just a question, and I don't want to risk starting out like that, knowing as I drive away that I am leaving them to think what I imagine they will think and then having to come back to them ten days from now.

And I do not tell them because I hardly know them and don't want to speak of this private thing between my father and me and whatever else is out there on the Plains, which may turn out to be nothing at all.

I thank them for the meal and good company, and they wish me safe travels as I go out the door. I have cousins. And they seem glad of me, which I note with a joy that is puzzling, this sense of relation, strange and new.

The map shows Minnesota dotted with blue lakes and ponds and enormous expanses of green in the north to show state and national forests. Spread out among them are boxy-looking territories marked as Indian reservations—Red Lake, Deer Creek, Leech Lake, Fond du Lac, Bois Forte, White Earth—outlined in the same color as wildlife refuges. It is hard not to notice what a small territory has been left to the People for whom the entire state and more were once their home.

To the south near the border with Iowa is the small town of Wells, at the junction of three roads, which might have lent it some importance once upon a time.

The road ahead is straight and flat, no hills or valleys, mile after mile of plowed fields on either side as far as I can see. And a scattering of trees that reminds me of driving west through Kansas on a speaking trip and asking my host how far you'd have to go to find enough trees in one place that a person could get lost in, and how she smiled when she said, "Colorado."

Every twenty miles or so a cluster of houses and a gas station/convenience store signal a town—Bird Island (pop. 1,195), Olivia, *Corn Capital of the World* (pop. 2,570), Buffalo Lake (pop. 764). The state highway is the main road through each town, with stubby streets branching out barely half a block on either side, where they end in fields to the south and to the north at railroad tracks running parallel to the road. After a while the towns seem attached to the rail line, like those fish that latch on to whales.

Here and there billboards are set in fields just off the road. One shows a white baby beside the words *My heart was beating 18 days after conception*, and then a little ways down the road, *Go ahead, hit the jackpot*, above the address for a Native American casino.

I am definitely from someplace other than here. But I am also not far from where my father was born and grew up.

Set out among the fields are clusters of tall shade trees—some at quite a distance—forming a collar closed on three sides against the winter wind, open only to the south. Huddled inside are a farmhouse, silo, and barn. The farms seem so far apart that I wonder how people make it through the winter, if they are lonely on the prairie.

In Granite Falls, a sign announces Chippewa County, the first specific mention of Native Americans aside from the casino. The road crosses the Minnesota River, gently sloping hills on either side.

I stop at a small grocery store for some crackers and fruit to eat along the way. In the checkout line I look for a pen to sign the receipt, and the clerk hands me a ballpoint with a long plastic spoon taped to the end, about a foot in length overall. I look down at it solemnly, then up at her, and say, "I promise I will not even try to steal this pen," and she smiles, and then I notice the woman behind me in line, middle-aged, round in a muscular, getting-through-the-day-no-matter-what kind of way, thick framed glasses, no-nonsense short hair, and she is suppressing a smile, not about to give in, something almost stoic about the way she pulls it off.

I am not invisible after all, I think, walking to the car, and then I happen to glance at the trunk and it occurs to me how easily I can forget, and I wonder what the people inside would think if they knew.

I open the door and slide into the driver's seat. Then again, maybe this is the kind of thing people do all the time, every day someone throwing a little box of ashes into a suitcase and flying off to see if they can find the right place to bury or scatter them or whatever else they feel inspired to do, including throwing them away. Maybe the woman in the line had just come from doing that very thing. Maybe behind the smile she was wondering how she'll ever understand Eastern types who cannot get over themselves long enough to do something as simple as taking proper care of a father's ashes. Maybe the only thing that makes me feel odd and out of place is my thinking that I am.

The road keeps crossing the Minnesota River, a sense of doubling back, covering the same ground again and again, like practice, or reincarnation, where you have to keep coming back until you get it right.

A little ways down the road, near Montevideo, a sign reads, "Historic marker, ½ mile on left," and I am wondering if I should stop, when suddenly there it is, and an irresistible impulse makes me swerve across a lane to make the turn into a driveway that curls among a scattering of trees. I park at the edge of an apron of mowed grass surrounding a forty- or fifty-foot spire made of rough-faced granite. "Camp Release" it says on one side, above a listing of battles—Redwood July 18, 1862, Fort Ridgley July 20–22, New Ulm July 23–24, Birch Cooley September 2, Fort Abercrombie September 6, Wood Lake September 23. Reading around the remaining sides, I realize that I am looking at a monument to the Dakota War, also known as Little Crow's War, but here referred to as the Great Sioux Indian Massacre.

I take my evening smoke in the shade of a nearby tree.

According to the text carved in stone, the war began with a massacre of whites. After losing the battle fought in this place, Wood Lake, a large band of Dakota surrendered with several hundred white captives, most of them women and children. Other Dakota fled north along the river.

I finish my smoke and leave a sprinkling of tobacco on the ground.

This was the end of the Dakota Sioux in Minnesota. The entire tribe was exiled to the west, including those who took no part in the war, who even urged against it and protected white people from harm.

The road is so straight and flat that it seems to offer no resistance, as if I could take my foot off the gas and coast all the way to South Dakota. Someone once speculated that one of the reasons Poland was so often invaded—whether by Cossacks on horseback or Germans in tanks—is the flat expanse of much of its terrain. Switzerland, on the other hand, even Hitler knew enough to leave alone.

I pass a cemetery dotted with flags and remember what day it is. I have seen no parades, nor even people except in the store in Granite Falls. And the man driving the huge rig of farm machinery coming at me now, hugging the far side of the road, truly enormous, something out of *Star Wars*, unlike anything I've ever seen.

I drive on, the light beginning to soften into evening. A small sign by the side of the road bids good-bye from the state of Minnesota, and South Dakota announces itself with billboards advertising fireworks for sale. I have crossed a line from one state to another, and yet everything seems the same except for the undulation of land about a meandering creek.

The hotel in Watertown is on the highway at the eastern end of a brightly lit strip of stores and gas stations and fast-food restaurants. On one side is a Walmart superstore, on another, a Chinese restaurant and a chiropractor, and on the third, the Prairie Rose Trading Post, selling a variety of things described as "boutique."

I unpack my bag and take a shower and brush my teeth and then spread the map out on the bed. The layout of eastern South Dakota reminds me of Iowa, with roads and county lines giving the appearance of having been assembled from blocks. To the west, shapes become irregular, distances more expansive, a tangle of rivers, lots of green, and much larger blocks of territory set aside for reservations—Standing Rock, Pine Ridge, Rosebud, Brulé, Crow Creek, Yankton. In the Pine Ridge reservation is a notation for Wounded Knee.

Hayti, where my father grew up and went to high school, is just south of here.

I get into bed and turn on the TV, even though I know it's a bad idea to seed my dreams with what I'm likely to find. Turning on a television in a room far from home is like comfort food, which may not be good for you but satisfies a need, or at least gives the impression of it.

A picture comes into view of children in a closet. I am watching *E.T. the Extra-Terrestrial.* I look over at the little brown box sitting in my open suitcase on the floor and think that what I need is one of those gizmos that Elliott has in the forest, scratching out a signal to the mother ship to come and bring both of us home. Except I don't know where that is or whether there even is a mother ship for us, or that maybe there is one for my father but not for me, like with Elliott when E.T. tells him he can't come with him and has to stay behind, and that the problem may not be getting a message out but being able to hear the one that's coming in.

But, then, as I watch the closing scene, I realize that in my longing I have rewritten the script, that I have it backwards, that it is E.T. who says, "Come?" and Elliot who says no. I am afraid that wherever my father has gone, I cannot follow, that where he belongs, I do not.

What if we are already home and I just don't know it, or there is a home somewhere but we cannot get there from here, or there was a long time ago but not anymore? What if we are so far displaced that there is no getting back?

I have no idea, pressing the button on the remote to mute the ads, except that we have come this far and we have barely begun, and my flight home doesn't leave for ten more days.

Looking out the window of my room, it is hard to imagine that all this concrete, steel, asphalt, and glass lie upon the seamless and continuous portion of the earth that I passed over yesterday. The view is jarring, of something broken into pieces that no longer fit together.

I go down to the lobby, where breakfast is laid out—waffles and bagels and pitchers of dry cereal and the ubiquitous bowl of red delicious apples, which are true to their name only in color but hold up so well they have become the unanimous choice of hotels around the country. I pour raisin bran into a Styrofoam bowl and find a seat at one of the small tables.

A large-screen TV is playing a sitcom that includes one of the few black faces I have seen since leaving home. Behind me, a row of video arcade games flanks the doorway into the pool area. Baskets of artificial philodendrons hang from a fake ceiling beam. A long corridor of guest rooms recedes like one of those dreams where no matter how fast you run, where you're trying to go keeps getting farther and farther away.

The black man on the TV is having a nightmare that he is about to be executed in an electric chair.

An elderly white couple sit down two tables from me and talk softly to each other, paying no attention to the TV. It is easier to do if you're not alone.

What is it about silence that it should be so hard to find? I once attended a Quaker Meeting for more than a year, drawn by the practice of sitting quietly and listening for the sound of Spirit coming in. I can think of no other place in this country where people come together to be in silence for almost any length of time. We avoid silence as if it were an opening through which bad things enter. Maybe it's true. "Stillness allows you to see what is," writes Mary Rose O'Reilly, and the more there is that you don't want to know, the more fearful the silence becomes.

The plastic spoon is too small for cereal, but it's what I've got. I eat slowly. I like to eat. Eating is good. It reminds me what I am.

It is 8:00 A.M. in Watertown, South Dakota, population 20,237, most of whom are of German or Norwegian ancestry. This is not a bad hotel. I have stayed in much worse. It is clean and the staff is friendly and eager to help, and people unknown to me are quick to say hello, which is more rare where I come from.

I finish eating and step outside into the chilly morning air. Low gray clouds cover the sky. American flags along the road are snapping in the wind coming from the east, which I notice since wind from that direction in New England often means a storm.

I imagine the people here are as good as anywhere else, maybe better, hardworking descendants of the people my grandfather came to minister to during the late 1920s and through most of the Great Depression. Living out on the prairie, the nearest large town fifty miles away, they probably stick together and have the kind of self-reliance that Americans like to think of as uniquely their own.

I wonder how the Depression affected life on reservations. Could they tell the difference?

I take my father's ashes from the suitcase and put them in my backpack. I would feel strange leaving him behind, even though any number of people I could name would assure me that it isn't him. Still, I cannot go off to Hayti while this box sits in a hotel room with people coming in with vacuum cleaners and mops and little carts of shampoo and soap. Him or not, that isn't something I can do. Besides, he is the reason I am here, and maybe he will be my divining rod when we're getting close. It may sound like a silly idea, but the fact is that none of us really know anything for sure and this is no time to be acting like I know what I'm pretty sure I do not.

I sit on the bed and eat one of the bananas I bought in Minnesota and then call the Lutheran church in Hayti to arrange an appointment with the pastor. His assistant says he's at his cottage on the lake, but if I come by at 9:30, he should be in.

I drive south on Route 81, rolling up the window against the cold. On the outskirts of Watertown, before the land shows itself again, is a huge complex of silos and buildings for turning corn into ethanol. All I can think of while driving by is the soaring price of food around the world and the four gallons of water it takes to make a single gallon of ethanol, which has to make you wonder why we keep hearing what a good idea it is, except for the ocean of money being poured into it by a government wanting to seem like it's doing something about the energy crisis, and farmers making more money than they have in quite a while.

The road is straight through flat, cultivated land. I turn west at Route 22, which I think is what she said, until I go through Thomas and see a sign for Hazel, which I remember from the map. I stop and turn around.

The sight of a lake reminds me of the little patches of blue on the map and my father saying how lucky he felt to have been in the 'lake country' of South Dakota. But there is something incongruous about the flatness of the land circling the shore, not like the hills I am used to, making it seem shallow and temporary, like puddles after a rain.

I turn south again on 81 and then west at the next road, where the sign reads, "Hayti, pop. 351." There is speculation about the naming of the town, some believing that Seymour Cole, the first postmaster, spent some time in Haiti while in the Navy, and it came from that. A rival theory is that it came from the practice of hay tying—tying hay in bundles used for fuel. And then there is the story that Mr. Cole simply closed his eyes and stuck his finger on a map of the world.

I don't know how many people lived here back in 1912, but I can guess it was about double what it is now, judging from what has happened to the population of Hamlin County, how quiet the land seems, so few people moving about. The number of farms has been dropping for a hundred years as small ones are gobbled up by bigger ones and young people cannot make a living at it and move away, leaving towns full of old people trying to remember what it was like before. There were more than a thousand farms in the county when my grandfather was here, but fewer than five hundred remain today.

It feels like a ghost town, although the people here might be offended to hear me say it. There are half a dozen short cross-hatched 'avenues' and streets lined with small frame houses, some better kept than others. The single main street runs east and west, with a collection of buildings at one end and the large brick county seat building at the other. There is a post office, a 24/7 fitness and tanning salon, a bowling alley, a barber shop, a provider of hand and foot care, a small grocery store, and the Lazy K Motel, with a handful of rooms and a large brightly colored children's play structure in the back. A few blocks away is a powder-blue water tower with HAYTI written across it. The avenues have names like Pioneer and Dakota, Flasher, Charger, and Pheasant, while the streets are numbered, like in New York.

The church is near the end of a residential street. I go inside and up a short flight of stairs, where the pastor's assistant welcomes me and shows me into an office across the hall. The pastor is young and earnest, fast-talking, friendly. I don't imagine he gets many visitors like me. I tell him about my father's dying and my wanting to know more about the places he had been, and the pastor warms to the subject, mentioning his love of history. His assistant appears at the door, and while they talk I look about the room, crowded with bookshelves and religious objects and mounted on the wall a set of antlers and a fanned-out turkey tail.

I ask him about the farms' being so far apart and are the people lonely because of it. He shakes his head and says the more spread out they are, the closer they become. They have church and holidays and events at the school. Then he smiles and says city people can be strangers living right on top of one another. Point taken.

I want to know what it is that binds people to the land. Native Americans see the land as sacred, I say, part of who they are, a matter of spirit. Is it that way here? No, he says, taking no time to think about it, he would not say it was a spiritual thing. It is ownership of the land that matters most to them. But they may be coming back to that, he says, the idea of the land belonging to God.

Just how far back was it left behind, I wonder, the idea that land belongs to God? I think to ask but he is off on something else with me trying to catch up, something about 'east river' and 'west river,' which turn out to mean east and west of the Missouri, which cuts the state in half on a rough diagonal. He is talking history now, reservations and land and flyers sent to the miserable people of Europe in the nineteenth century, posted in churches and public squares to advertise land in the 'New World,' free to anyone willing to live and work on it. They came in droves, Germans, Dutch, Scandinavians, imported to drive out the Indians and clear the land for investors and robber barons looking to get rich on railroads and mining and timber and for politicians after statehood.

We sit in silence for a while and then I remember where I am and ask what Jesus would have made of this.

He says he doesn't think Jesus would have liked it at all, the kingdom of God being about equality and fairness, justice, love.

Then, I ask, how do you reconcile building a nation on stolen land?

He pauses, looking out the window, and then says it was a long time ago and you cannot steal what people do not think they own.

I wonder to myself, if the land belongs to God, then is owning it a presumption, an affront, and is stealing it a desecration?

The earliest white settlers, among whom were my ancestors on my mother's side, at first acknowledged an absolute Native American right to the land, something Native Americans could not morally be compelled to give up. It is plain to see in their writings and letters. And yet the settlers did exactly that, often with a vengeance that shocked the 'savage' tribes who might ally with them for some temporary advantage. The settlers were people who put great stock in their Christian faith, so how could they not have known what they were doing? And, if they did know, what am I to make of that now? Who *were* they? And who, then, am I, descended from them?

We have been talking for most of an hour when I ask about the trees.

Every one you see out here was planted by white people, he says, and before that, it was all grassland and prairie.

So, I ask, what if a person wanted to go where there are no trees?

He points a thumb back over his shoulder and says you go sixty, a hundred miles to the west. He makes a little smile and says out there the farms are *really* far apart.

The conversation drifts. We talk about trees and prairie. I ask about the reservation above Watertown.

He says you'd never know that's what it is. It looks like anywhere else, white people everywhere. If you want to see a real reservation, go to Rosebud or Pine Ridge.

How far is that? I ask.

Real far.

I park on Main Street and take some photographs from either end. I would go out of my mind in a place like this. Empty storefronts, a sense of desolation and displacement, the irony of the greed that drove Native Americans from the land playing no favorites, whites now being driven off by other whites.

I drive around, passing by where the high school used to be, the site now marked by a sign. I try to picture my father living here, the man who traveled the world and spoke four languages and had suits made in London and Hong Kong, who played the piano and violin and had a master's degree in music and could teach any orchestral instrument but the harp. The town must have been fuller and more vital then, eighty years ago, but still, it is so small and far away from anything reminiscent of him that it's hard to imagine that who he was came out of here.

I drive south on 81 and then over to Lake Norden, where there used to be a church where my grandfather preached, serving more than one town as pastors often did, since no town was big enough to support one by itself. The church was abandoned and torn down in 1937 and the materials sold to the Lutheran church in Hayti, a consolidation of souls that went along with what was happening on the land.

I turn north on a secondary road, the sadness of no place for my father coming over me again. And then I wonder what it is that makes me so sure this is not the one.

The next road east will take me back to 81.

It is not the place, because there is nothing left behind that would connect him to it beyond a few stories about passing through on his way out of the flat Midwest to the mountains and the ocean that he loved the moment he first saw them. But that does not mean the mountains and the ocean are where he was from or where he belongs.

The pastor mentioned a man raising buffalo a few miles down Route 81, so I turn south at the crossroads.

It makes sense that the place where you are from must also be the place where your People are from. So, who are my father's People?

Such a simple question, but then why don't I answer it, instead of driving down the road and looking into fields, trying to tell the difference between a black cow and a buffalo?

I feel annoyed at how difficult this is, or how difficult I am already making it.

I would have liked to see a buffalo. If there are any down this way, they are not where I can see them.

My father's People are his family, but where are they? His children, grandchildren, and great-grandchildren are in western Canada, Massachusetts, California, Connecticut, and Ontario. He lived out his retirement with my stepmother in the state of Washington, but now she lives in Connecticut near us. His parents are buried in Minnesota, and his grandparents in Iowa. Everyone else, going back just about forever, is in Norway, so if you do the math and figure the weight, that must be the place. This has occurred to me before, of course, since he made it clear that a Norwegian is what he was.

I turn around and drive north again.

He was a Norwegian who was also American, although not really, not quite, not exactly, and yet also without a doubt.

When I visited Norway with my father in 1993, I was surrounded by Norwegians and all things Norwegian, and there was a moment, far down toward the end of Hardangerfjord, where so many of my ancestors lived their lives, when a feeling came over me that I think I will always remember as the first time I knew what it might be like to know where I was from. I was standing on the hillside leading down to the water, looking at the mountains on the other side, when there was a stillness and then a softening around my heart, a letting down of something I had been holding against my whole life perhaps, and then an almost indescribable sense of ease, the complete absence of resistance to being wholly in this place, as if I had always been here and to be somewhere else in that moment was beyond imagining. It was so simple, this feeling, as if every breath bore the silent affirmation, *oh, yes, of course.*

And then it was gone almost as soon as it appeared, and I went back to being a displaced American among people who never imagined themselves as anything but Norwegian and who were, in that, not like me at all.

If Norwegians are not my People, then how could they be my father's? How could there be such a break between us?

A few drops of rain fall on the windshield, a feeling coming in of disappointment and not knowing where I am.

You make a plan to get you to a place where the plan can fall apart, and then picking through the pieces you find what you didn't see before. It is just past 3:00 in the afternoon, and I am bored and restless and want to go home. I would have a smoke, but it's too early, or I could eat something, but what then?

I drive to the Historical Museum in the center of Watertown. The building is old and made of stone and according to the words above the door was one of the public libraries funded by Andrew Carnegie's philanthropy. Carnegie emigrated from Scotland in 1848 and went on to make a fortune first in railroads and then in steel, which he could not have done without the iron ore on Native American land or without millions of acres of right-of-way handed over by the government free of charge or without masses of immigrant labor willing to work under any conditions and for almost nothing at all, not to mention millions of enslaved black people in the South whose free labor formed the backbone of the American Industrial Revolution.

Carnegie became one of the wealthiest men in the world—worth almost $300 billion in today's dollars—who in his later years devoted himself to giving most of it away to promote education and peace. He was the kind of man my parents would admire, hardworking and 'self-made,' educated and successful and acting for the common good. And they would no doubt be impatient with the mixed emotions running through me as I stand here looking up at his name and wondering both at what he achieved and what it cost generations of human beings who had no say in how he got it or what he did with it once he had it.

Inside the museum is a cozy, almost intimate space. An elderly woman at the front desk says a cheery hello and asks me to sign the register. I look about to get my bearings, knowing right away that this won't take very long. There are displays of military uniforms from various wars, helmets and posters (buy bonds!), an assortment of books for sale, cards with portraits of Native Americans; an interior of a Victorian house in town, with furniture and dishes on the table, mannequins dressed in period clothing; artifacts of individuals and families who came from somewhere else barely a hundred years ago in order to make a life. This much they had in common, but having a similar purpose is not the same as having a common one, which I do not see here, the history of a People.

I go back to the hotel and am having my evening smoke, leaning against the wall facing the Walmart across the way, when I remember something the pastor said this morning, that there was a war over land and the Indians lost and that's just the way it went.

Things merely happen—right out of Ecclesiastes, a time for everything, a rock at the edge of a hill for a thousand years and then one day set in motion for no apparent reason and winding up where it does because, well, that's just how it went. *Shit happens.*

And with a simple rhetorical shrug he managed to make it all go away, if only for a second or two, which might have gone on longer if I were not so aware of my father's ashes out in the car.

I wish I did not have them now, that they had not come to me, that I could just put them down and walk away. He said it didn't matter, after all, *makes no difference*, and then looking away, that shrug, what I also felt in the pastor this morning and what I see now in the pavement and buildings and plowed-up fields where once there was grass and prairie as far as you could see and sixty million buffalo and entire nations whose presence here goes back tens of thousands of years. That shrug of a museum this afternoon with its nostalgia for war and the westward 'expansion' and brave pioneers who just happened to come to a place that just happened to be the land of someone else. It does not *matter*, it makes no *difference*, because we are so displaced ourselves that we cannot see past what we want and need and all the rest, what comes after, just *happens*. Whole cultures are made to disappear, entire Peoples made invisible, and sacred land turned into an industrial resource, a piece of property, the object of title deeds and boundary stakes and portfolios. The buffalo and the elk are all but gone, and now we have islands of concrete and macadam and steel and blazing light in the middle of the prairie and small towns all but emptied out and ethanol plants running twenty-four hours a day.

I put out the cigarette beneath my shoe. I want something more to matter, something larger and more enduring than property and ownership and who won. I do not want this to be what I am from, who I am.

Upstairs in my room, I make a bowl of oatmeal in the microwave and eat it with a piece of fruit. It isn't much, but it's all I want. When I picture myself going to a restaurant and imagine the food on the plate, I cannot bring myself to eat, as if it isn't real.

There is still some light in the sky when I start the car and point it north along the highway and then take the first exit, which, according to the map, will shortly put me in the middle of the Lake Traverse Reservation, home to the Sisseton and Wahpeton bands of the Dakotah-Nakota-Lakota Nation, known to white people as the Sioux. Before setting out I went online and came across a man by the name of Ed Red Owl who lives on the reservation. "The real significance of *Dakotah*," he writes, "derives from *WoDakotah*, which means harmony, a condition of being at peace with oneself and in harmony with one another and with nature." The territory of the Wahpetonwan—'people dwelling among the leaves'—and the Sissetonwan—'people of the fish villages'—extended from Canada down through Minnesota and into northern Iowa until they were exiled by white people following the Dakota War in 1862, just two years before my great-grandfather left the sea and came to Chicago at the age of twenty-five.

Before my ancestors came, there was no such place as Minnesota or Iowa or Canada.

Several years ago at the White Privilege Conference in Colorado Springs, I met a Native American man whose tribe lives in what is now

Alberta. I asked him which he would prefer, to be Native American in Canada or the United States. He thought for a moment, then smiled and said, "North America."

A cold raw wind out of the east brings rain. The land going by looks much like everywhere else, flat cultivated fields, the occasional farmhouse and barn. A weathered sign points west to the Dakota Sioux Casino. I stop the car, back up, and take the turn.

The casino appears suddenly over a gentle rise in the road, a large rectangular solid of light brown stone fronted in glass several stories high. A brightly colored border runs around the top, and to the left above the canopied entrance is a structure in the shape of a tepee with lower panels depicting buffalo and other forms and seven poles rising toward the apex, torches for each of the bands of the Dakotah-Lakota-Nakota Nation.

There is a gas station and a hotel and a parking lot half-full of cars, and farmland stretching out to the horizon. I park and go inside.

The first person I see is the Native American woman behind the counter in the lobby. She reminds me of Marilyn in *Northern Exposure.* She glances up at me and then looks back down at what she is doing and I am suddenly aware of being white, an experience I have had before but not often enough to get used to it. It is more than feeling odd and out of place. It is to trespass, as in *who are you and what are you doing here,* not a question but a naming wrapped in a challenge, *we know who you are.* And yet as I look around, there is not an unfriendly or unwelcoming face that I can see. Which, of course, doesn't necessarily mean a thing. I am a customer, and a white man to boot. What do I expect?

Trespass and guilt. When the subject of guilt comes up, I often tell audiences that there is nothing more useless than a guilty white person. So, here I am, the tall white guy trying to look nonchalant as he walks across the lobby and into the casino, like he knows exactly where he is and what he's doing.

There is a middling collection of people scattered among the gambling machines. As far as I can tell, all of them are white. I move through rows of blinking lights and the bings and bongs of the machines, feeling the irony of a place where white people come to pour their money into the pockets of Native Americans, a siphon drawing blood, bleeding as a cure, *step this way, it won't hurt a bit, it might even be fun and, who knows, you might even be a winner,* the colors dazzling and bright like the beads that bought Manhattan. We were gamblers when we first came, and we are gamblers still.

On my way out I pass two young Native American women leaning against the wall and having a smoke, on a break. They smile and nod as I go by, and I smile and nod in return and have to make myself walk slowly, because a part of me I had not known about wants only to get out the door and into the air and be in my car on the road heading south to my warm little room at the Super 8 Hotel with the Walmart out the back.

I kick off my shoes and lie down on the bed and turn on the TV. There is a documentary on Frank Sinatra and then an ad for the film *Fort Apache,* "the undying story of courage and romance carved out of the nation's pioneer heritage." Henry Fonda delivers ultimatums to Cochise and John Wayne swears he will never break his word. I grew up on stories like these, and back then I always wanted the white people to win. I did not think of them as white, did not use the word, just the good guys, the ones who looked like me, even Errol Flynn as Custer in *They Died with Their Boots On.* I wanted them not only to win but also to be good, which meant the Indians had to be treacherous and bad, with just enough noble exceptions to make it interesting.

I turn the channel. Another movie, white people on a ship and, judging by the clothes, the 1930s. Faye Dunaway, Oskar Werner, Lee Grant all going to Cuba with a sense of dread in the air, and I know this ship and its story, which really happened, a thousand Jews in 1939 fleeing Nazi Germany aboard the SS *St. Louis* out of Hamburg bound for Havana, turned away by the Cubans, sailing north to the United States only to be turned away again and then sent back to Europe and what for most of them will be death in the concentration camps.

I watch the last hour of the film in spite of knowing how it ends, or perhaps because of it. Last night it was *E.T.* and now this story of people in search of a place where they can belong. And be saved.

It is not lost on me, what keeps showing up on the TV, like dreams except that I'm awake.

I like being out here on my own, solitary, autonomous, no one knowing my name, where I am from. I like the sense of ease in being able to come and go as I please, unattached, not having to explain what I'm doing here. As if I have the right. Is this the pioneer spirit of my ancestors, what enabled them to do what they did to make a place for themselves in a strange land that belonged to someone else? Am I more like them than I know?

Bent over my bowl of cereal, I try to ignore the television on the far side of the lobby. I manage for a little while, but there is something so relentless about the ads and game shows that bits and pieces get in just the same.

I want it all and I want it now

Real people, big money

I hurry breakfast and go upstairs to eat a banana in the quiet of my room.

I will drive west today until there are no more trees.

I can tell I am far from home by the billboards

the cost of an abortion is a human life

a theme that crops up every dozen miles or so. And then, coming into a town

fur and pheasant country
activists not welcome

I don't have to be an animal rights activist to feel this is directed at me. It is the outsider in me that resonates, feeling unwelcome and unsafe.

My destination is the town of Zell, partly because I like the name but also because it is eighty miles from Watertown, splitting the difference between the sixty to one hundred miles the pastor said it would take to get beyond the trees. The land is flat, the road straight, only the occasional car or truck going by, leaving my mind plenty of room to wander.

In 1901, my grandfather was ordained and came west to Great Falls, Montana, to begin his preaching career. It was more than a thousand miles across what had been the land of Lakota and Cheyenne, and he would have gone by train, the Northern Pacific, across South Dakota. I imagine him rocking to the motion of the car, gazing out the window at the same prairie all around me now. I wonder if he felt the sorrow in this place, sorrow for the massacre at Wounded Knee and the murder of Sitting Bull just eleven years before, sorrow for a People driven from the land, for millions of buffalo shot from the windows of passing trains and left to rot in the sun for the sole purpose of making the ancient life of the Plains Indians impossible.

I am remembering what the pastor said of Jesus and wondering how my grandfather's calling affected what he knew and felt about what was done. Did being a Christian put him on the side of God's kingdom of justice and love? Or was he more like the missionaries who often led the way in persuading Native Americans to give up their land?

I do not know what my grandfather thought or felt. He may have just stared down into his Bible or daydreamed about his life. Or he may have wept as he gazed out the window. What I do know is that he was once where I am now and that I am connected to more than I can know, my life unfolding as a story intersecting with the stories of people I have never known, long since dead, yet to be born, played out against a larger story present to me now beneath an enormous sky.

It is an absence that I feel in the openness all around me, the sense of all that is not here, the emptiness left behind when entire nations of people are forced to leave their country, banished completely and forever. I try to imagine what a catastrophe that would be, which I realize is what I am driving through, the unmarked scene of an utter disaster of body and soul.

I have always been living in the midst of it. I just did not know until now.

And it did not merely *happen* but was planned and done, some of it in my grandfather's time, a fact of his existence just as the Vietnam War and the wars since have been facts of my own.

The People of this place for whom the land was sacred and holy are still here, and yet they have been made invisible, except for the casual appropriation of words and images to name, among other things, white towns and white counties and white states and white rivers and white mountains, sentimentalized and distorted and stripped of meaning from the lives of the People they refer to. When I was growing up and studying geography in school, 'Dakota' and 'Massachusetts' and 'Iowa' were presented as American names for places in America, words in the English language, that being the language of this place. 'Dakota' as the name of a nation does not appear in my unabridged dictionary until the fourth definition, so a boy growing up might be forgiven for not knowing what it was.

I pull off to the side of the road on the near side of Zell (pop. 79), and unfold my map of South Dakota over the steering wheel. There is a small patch of green just below the capital city of Pierre, the National Grassland, abutting the Lower Brulé and Crow Creek reservations. However far I have come, it is not far enough to feel that I am seeing the land as it was, as close as I can get to the time before white people came and plowed under the grass and killed the buffalo and planted trees and drove the First People away. I trace the route and figure it is 150 miles from Zell and then 250 more back to my hotel for the night, 500 miles in all.

Nora would shake her head and smile to see me now, folding up the map and starting the car and pulling back onto the road on my way to Pierre. The man she knows would balk at a spontaneous suggestion to tack another three hundred miles onto the day—too far, too long, too much driving, getting back too late, *blah blah blah.*

Part of the difference is that I am alone and it is my idea. But there is something else, a letting go into a place inside myself I have not known before, where time and distance seem not to matter, my body immune to the ache and stiffness from sitting for hours in the seat of a car, as if I were floating down a river that carries me along and all I have to do is steer.

Fifty miles from Pierre—which they pronounce 'Peer,' even though the name comes from a French fur trapper—coming into Hyde County, plowed fields giving way to grass, farms to ranches. There are black cattle and a sign for a place called Ree Heights (pop. 85), off to the south, a long low rise in the land, the first thing like a hill I've seen in days. The road is straight in front of me, running west, the skyline unbroken except for the line of telephone poles receding in the distance, crossing beneath the high power lines running north to south, the huge towers marching like robots across the land.

I encounter my first real hill—where the car has to shift down a gear to make the climb—in the town of Harrold (pop. 209). I pass a historical marker and stop and turn around to have a look. It was put up in 1882 and tells the story of the first white settlers, making the point that railroads got here first. The settlers were never far behind, lured by pamphlets and posters sent out by railroad magnates spreading the news of the Homestead Act and promising free land for growing crops the railroads would haul to market.

There is no mention of how the land came to be available to white people wanting to build railroads and graze cattle, as if it were just empty and here for the taking. No mention of the war that raged across western South Dakota and Montana and Wyoming in the years following the Civil War. Nothing about the Indians fighting back against white settlers and miners invading their land under the protection of the U.S. Army. Nor does it say that in 1868 the Native People won, the army forts abandoned and burned to the ground and the Black Hills guaranteed to the victors in perpetuity.

Walking back to the car, it comes to me that while all this was taking place, my great-grandfather was sailing on the Great Lakes and working to become an American who would be encouraged to feel that some portion of this land was his own.

Pierre is small as capital cities go, just under fourteen thousand people, the second smallest behind Montpelier, Vermont. It has trees, unlike the prairie all around.

Not wanting to take up a lot of time to eat, I stop at the first fast-food place I can find and buy a sandwich and sit at a small table in the corner in the middle of a lunch-hour crowd. There is a white couple sitting in the booth across the aisle, and I ask them for directions to the National Grasslands. They tell me how to get there, and then the woman asks if I'm going there to hunt, and when I shake my head, they smile in a friendly way but with the subtle and yet unmistakable look of someone who thinks they've pretty much figured out what sort of person you are. And maybe they have.

I finish my meal and drive across the Missouri River before turning south. There are houses perched on high naked bluffs to the west, the land looking scraped and raw and the buildings out of place, as if glued there by a child in a hurry, no roots and barely hanging on.

The city falls away behind me, and then I am looking at the beginning of something I have never seen, a vast rolling expanse of prairie free of everything but grass, beneath a sky full of low gray clouds, soft and still. I drive on, not quite knowing what to do.

Just past a sign announcing the interstate up ahead, I pull off the road and stop the car. At first I think it is to turn around before the sight of a super highway spoils my memory of this place. But then, slowly, it comes to me that to the south and west, beyond the highway, are the Pine Ridge and Rosebud Lakota Sioux reservations.

Until just now, I had not imagined that I might come this far, to be so close to the place and the People I have read about so many times. It had not occurred to me that my father's story would lead me here. I sit in the car and feel the shudder of large trucks barreling past, picturing in my mind, over there, beyond the horizon, the cemetery at Wounded Knee. Over there is where white soldiers murdered hundreds, mostly women and children and old men, in the snow more than a hundred years ago. But it is also the place where in 1973 the American Indian Movement defied the federal government with an armed occupation that lasted more than two months, demanding that the United States live up to its treaty obligations. Over there are the People who still demand the return of the sacred Black Hills, which the U.S. Supreme Court ruled had been illegally taken from them. Over there are the People who are still fighting to reclaim the identity and way of life that was all but taken from them and to survive some of the worst poverty on this continent. Over there are not the Native Americans frozen in the past whom most white people imagine from movies and books and highway monuments and markers, caricatures of the noble sage and warrior appropriated by advertisers and sports teams. These are not a vanished People but living human beings who are still here in spite of our best efforts to make them disappear, because, in spite of all, they have somehow managed to make themselves hard to kill.

I take out the map and spread it open on the steering wheel. The reservations are more than a hundred miles away. I close my eyes in the presence of a need to put myself in that place, to go to Wounded Knee. I don't care that it's too far, that I don't have time, that I have places to go, hotels and people expecting me on such and such a day. I want to go there, now.

But I do not make a move to start the car, because I am also in the presence of fear, an urgency to turn around and go back the way I came.

Of what am I afraid?

I am afraid of going to a place where I not only do not belong but also have no right to be, which anyone I meet will tell me by the way they look at me. *You take everything from us, you push us onto these reservations, land you do not want, and even here we are not safe from you.* It will not matter what is in my politics or my heart. For all my good intentions, they will have no reason to trust or welcome me. All they will see is another white man in a rental car come to observe, a tourist looking for the exotic, a sociologist, perhaps, wanting to study the tragedy of their desperate condition and write a book about it. Or some New Age seeker looking for relief from the loneliness and emptiness and despair that come of generations of forgetting how to live on the earth.

I play in my head a conversation in which I try to make clear my grief and anger over what was done to them and is still done, my years of study and teaching, writing, and speaking about white privilege, my alienation from white culture and its violence against the earth, my search for what it means to live as a human being, not only for myself but also as an offering to Spirit and generations yet to come.

But why are you here? they want to know, and I cannot think of what to say. Except to escape, to find some refuge, if only for a while, from the impossibility of being a white man who knows what I know and can still believe that he belongs in North America. Or anywhere.

I lose track of time as I sit and stare at the horizon, and then I start up the car and turn around.

Driving north, I see a small pond down a gentle slope by the side of the road. I stop the car and sit for a while, looking out across the land. The car trembles from trucks going by.

I get out and walk down into the grass, the road rising up behind me, sheltering me from the noise of traffic. The old grass is the color of cut hay mixed in with new. There are yellow flowers and purple and birdsong all around, although I cannot see the birds, making it seem as though the grass itself is singing as it bends before the wind. I walk down and down, turning every once in a while to look back up at the car as if for reassurance, uneasy at being barely able to see it now, but still I move forward and let myself descend into what seems another place, another kind of being. When I turn around, I cannot see the car. I am being swallowed by a stillness of land and grass.

I walk down to the pond and stand there for a while, watching ducks and geese.

Years ago I could have said from the knowledge in my mind that to stand on the land where I am standing now is to stand on Lakota land, Cheyenne, and Crow, and many others, but now the weight of it is coming into my body for the first time in a deeper measure of what it means for this to be true.

Imagine the Sahara Desert, rounded contours of sand in all directions as far as you can see. Imagine standing in the middle of all of that and turning slowly in a circle to open yourself to the vastness of it, how full a stillness can be. And then cover all of it with grass in a hundred shades of green and yellow and brown all mixed together, and that is what I am seeing now.

My eyes keep filling up, moved beyond words by what I can only imagine First People see and feel when they stand here and look out over the kind of land from which visions come if you sit with it long enough. And then comes the grief that I will never do more than imagine this, raised in a culture that would have me see nothing here but a beautiful 'empty' and 'undeveloped' and 'unpopulated' space.

I am not from here, but, if we go back far enough, we are all from someplace like it, the hush of an ageless repose, ever changing and undisturbed. We are all from a First People, an Original People, if only we knew who they were, if we could walk the land where they were the indigenous ones. In theory, I can locate such places on a map, but not in the geography of my heart, and in this my father cannot help me find my way. Unless he already has and left the rest to me.

I turn off the highway and head southeast on route 1806, named for the year that Lewis and Clark passed this way and first encountered the Teton Sioux. There are redwing blackbirds and pheasants and quail by the side of the road and cattle on a ridgeline silhouetted against the sky.

A building appears, the Buffalo Interpretive Center, run by the Lower Brulé Sioux, the *Kul Wicasa Oyate*, a band of the Lakota Nation. There are no cars in the parking lot, and I am wondering if it's closed when I notice a young man tending the vegetation. I feel awkward getting out of the car, conscious of my white self coming here, even though I was invited by the sign at the beginning of the road, *The Native American Scenic Byway*, and the sign over the door, by the parking lot. I am the white tourist they were expecting, even counting on. But there is also the history that calls for a place like this, which I have no doubt that he knows as he waits for the white man in his rental car to come along and show an interest in what white people did their best to destroy.

He unlocks the door and leads me inside, turning on lights as we go. There is an area of gifts and books and beyond that a large room with an exhibit of life on the Plains as it was. He tells me there is a short video about the buffalo and that I should let him know when I am ready to see it. He is not unfriendly but reserved as he goes back to sit behind the counter.

I watch videos on touch screens showing the making of a tipi, the building of a fire, traditional children's games. The room seems enormous with no one in it but me and him, waiting for me to do whatever I am going to do. There is no crowd to disappear in, no flow of people coming and going, just the exhibits and the weight of history and me in here and him out there aware of each other.

I tell him I am ready and go into the next room where there is a screen on the wall and benches. I sit in the middle toward the front. There are signs on either side of the screen with phrases in Lakota and in English, greetings, the language of everyday life.

The video begins, about bringing back the buffalo, not just to eat, which they do only once in a while, but more to remind the People of who and where they are.

When the video is done, I sit in the silence of the darkened room until I am aware of him outside in the lobby, waiting for me so that he can get back to work outside.

I go and thank him and take out my wallet and give him the money for the entrance fee. He takes it and walks me to the door, turning out the lights on the way.

Sitting in the car, I wonder if I should have given more. And if I had, what do I imagine would have changed between us, and who would it be for.

I look at my backpack on the floor. What am I doing here? What do I think I am going to find in this place? How much have I missed already because I do not know how to see?

I did not think to ask him about the term for all the tribes together. There are problems no matter what you do. 'Indians' is insulting, going back to Columbus, who thought he was where he was not. 'American Indian' doubles the insult, since white people have never treated them as real Americans. 'Native American' is widely used but turns out to have been invented by the Bureau of Indian Affairs as a way to diminish the people it names by suggesting they are no different from other hyphenated Americans, just one more ethnic group added to the pot.

'I' do not know what name to use for 'them.'

I do not want to admit that I am annoyed at having to think about it, the annoyance of the conqueror who presumes the right to name everything and have it stick without having to think of it again, the plant, the mountain, the river, the People becoming what we name them and the image that we carry in our minds as part of the story we use to tell ourselves who we are.

This is who I am, embarrassed by my complicity.

I stop the car and get out and walk a few steps down the slope and sit. How am I to be here and not think of them, and how am I to think of them without a name?

There are those who favor 'Indigenous,' 'Original,' and 'First People,' but then come the arguments about how many thousands of years you have to go back to establish just who they were and how they are related and to whom. And who decides?

Is 'Indigenous' or 'Original' a matter of science or something closer to the soul, and when the soul seeks after itself, does it look into the sky, toward some kind of heaven, or is it looking into the earth that I am sitting on?

I close my eyes. Open my eyes. And it comes to me that there has never been a sky I would remember for the rest of my life. There has never been a sky—including the sky on a clear night viewed through a telescope at the top of a mountain outside Tucson, Arizona—that left me speechless and still, unable to think, even to *see*, as I am right now, it being everything I can do just to be in the presence of whatever is emanating from the land all around me, the sound of the wind moving through the grass, around my face. Why is it that I will never forget the Grand Canyon? Or being in the middle of the ocean? Or this? And every time it is the same, the stillness, the hush, like prayer, a state of grace.

Perhaps 'Indigenous' is a landed condition of being, which is why I am not indigenous to this place where I am now and will never be, nor my father or my children or all the children who come after. I do not know exactly why it is, but the body may know what the mind cannot explain.

Two hundred years ago, I would have seen a million buffalo darkening the plain, moving like the shadow of a cloud. Over there, to the west 150 miles or so, are the Black Hills, *Paha Sapa*, sacred to the

Lakota, guaranteed forever by the government of the United States, forbidden to white people until they changed their minds in 1874, when my great-grandparents were establishing their farm in Iowa, 350 miles to the east.

Driving through the village of Lower Brulé, I notice names of streets—Two Hawks, Splintered Horn, Red Cloud, Medicine Bull, Omaha, Little Elk, Sacred Circle—at once sacred and mundane, every place *some* place, more than an address or coordinates on a map, significant beyond what it seems or what can be taken from it or what it's worth or will be to someone someday.

The People did not understand the European idea of owning land, inconceivable, like owning a piece of God. And there was a time in Europe—if you go back far enough—when indigenous people there felt pretty much the same way. But not anymore, and once you think of God as something you can own, what becomes of you then?

The land turns back to farms beneath small patches of blue showing through the clouds. I have been thinking about names and naming for the better part of a hundred miles, passing through one town after another with names like Miller and Wessington and trying to connect the names with the ethnic origins of the people who live there, mostly German and Norwegian. And yet you would never know it by the names, just as New York is a city full of people from anywhere but England, which makes me wonder if there is a name for any place in this country that tells you anything true about the people living there.

And then there is the movement to make English the official language of the United States. Since language is what most identifies a People in ethnic terms, are we then English? And yet, if you look at a map of the United States based on how people classify themselves, the largest ethnic group in most counties is German, with Mexican, African American, and 'American' far behind. 'American' counties turn out to be a mix of English, French, Welsh, Scottish, and Irish, and counties dominated by those who identify as English are few and far between, mostly in Vermont, New Hampshire, Maine, and Utah.

At the junction of Route 25 north is the town of De Smet and signs pointing out its connection with the family of Laura Ingalls Wilder, author of *Little House on the Prairie.* It turns out I've been driving on the Laura Ingalls Wilder Historic Highway, which goes on for quite a ways into Minnesota. She is something of a sensation out here. It's hard to get away from her. It's also hard to imagine how many millions of young people have learned most of what they know about the settling of the West from Wilder's books. If I had known about them as a boy, I am sure I would have read them all and enjoyed every one, along with the biographies of Kit Carson and Wild Bill Hickock that I read beneath the covers at night. I would have appreciated how hard it was to make a life in places like this, families all alone on the prairie, having to do everything for themselves and with all the things there were to be afraid of, and that sense of being a child looking to your parents to protect and take care of you.

And I would have believed every word, each reference to 'Indians' and 'savages' who have no more right to the land than do wild animals, treaties or not, the natural succession of white people coming in and Indians moving out, like summer giving way to fall, 'good' Indians being friendly and looking out for whites, even defending them against 'bad' Indians who presume to believe they have a right to put up a fight.

Turning east, the sky darkening above me and sadness coming in, like a bit of weather, the five hundred miles stretching out behind me at the end of a long day, my father's ashes still sitting in my backpack with no place to go. I feel as though I am trying to raise the dead, bring back something that is so long gone I don't know what it is or was or could have been.

I eat and shower and get into bed, turning on the TV to see what it has to offer me tonight. *The Manchurian Candidate.* All these stories of being lost, unable to find your way home, the perils of forgetting who you are.

I turn off the TV and open the novel I brought along to ease me over the hump into sleep. I don't know why it comes to me, something in the story, but I remember asking my father about when he was growing up, was he aware of a Native American presence in his life, the history of the place, of reservations, with one just up the road from Hayti. And he said no, not that he could recall.

How can that be?

And yet, how long does it take to forget if no effort is made to remember?

Then I am thinking about tomorrow and my trip back across Minnesota to where my father was born, and I remember how Camp Release pulled me off the road like a magnet. I am beyond tired, but the day is not over. I climb out of bed, put on my clothes, and go downstairs to the computer in the lobby to find out what I can about the Dakota War of 1862.

The only fragment I am able to retrieve from the dream that I was dreaming when I woke up this morning is the sight of land. Perhaps it was not a fragment, but the whole, what I came looking for. I look out the window at misty rain and fog and feel again the ancient repose in a land covered with grass, a waiting to receive, but unable to see what it will take for my father and me to be received here or anywhere.

I dress and pack and take my things down to the car before eating breakfast to the sound of the TV in the lobby. I look around at the handful of people in the room, no one paying attention to the television.

Anyone mind if I turn this off?

Shaking heads all around.

The first time I ever did that. I wonder why. And what else is there that I do not say, even to myself?

"It was so long ago," the pastor said, the war against Native Americans. But was it really? Is it even past? Is our history not here with us now? Are we not living a national nightmare driven by the same forces that drove white people then, the fear, the uncertainty, the grasping for more? Are we to believe this all came out of the blue?

I drive east toward Minnesota, the air still thick with fog.

Or is this just some white liberal angst that I am going through, a self-inflicted wound, *get over it*, the voice in my head, and yes, it was bad, but not *that* bad. Nothing worse than what they did to one another all the time.

Or, it could not have been that bad, because if it was, how would anyone have stood it? How do you construct a national imagination, a collective remembering that turns this into something bad but not so bad as to show itself so that everyone knows that everyone knows and there is no escape.

Welcome to Minnesota

I notice the word 'tragedy' in descriptions of what happened here, as in something terrible that can't be helped, Oedipus murdering his father and marrying his mother and putting out his eyes. I am strangely comforted by the word, how it frees me to feel bad for a while and then walk away and leave it behind, no need to qualify or argue, defend myself, even get upset. I can feel bad without doubting my own goodness, reminding myself that I am not callous or unfeeling. I am a man who knows tragedy when he sees it, not the sort who could do such things himself or be descended from anyone who would. And even if they did way back then, it could not be helped, what happened, it being just the way it was. *There was a war over land and the Indians lost*, like a tree falling across the road or a car going out of control.

I am glancing at the sky and wishing the sun would show itself when I am suddenly aware that I cannot remember the precise motion of putting my backpack in the car, and I think that I've forgotten it, my father's ashes and all my notes left somewhere in the parking lot, the image flashing through my mind in less time than it takes for me to glance down into the foot well and see yes, it is there, right where I put it, and I can feel my heart beating in my chest as I wonder what could make me so afraid.

The fog thins as I pass through Granite Falls and turn east and then south on Route 67, going by the Upper Sioux Reservation, a small heavily wooded patch of land with a sign that reads, "Use of recreational facilities for tribal members only."

Driving on, the land opens up again to an unobstructed view of the horizon that reminds me of the middle of the ocean, which I remember from going to Norway when I was six years old.

There was so much land that tribes could push each other around, but always knowing there was enough, that no one was being driven to extinction, because the point was never to take it all, that being impossible, unimaginable that anyone would be able or inclined to do such a thing.

Until the Europeans came and it was impossible to know how many were still to come from over the horizon, like an invasive weed that just keeps coming until it is everywhere and pushes out everything else. And believing all the while in ownership and private property and accumulation and profit, making a virtue of excess.

In Redwood Falls I come upon a strip of fast-food restaurants, tacos and burgers and fried chicken, and then as I turn south on Route 2, it all falls away, and there is a sign welcoming me to the Lower Sioux Community and I feel as if I have crossed into another country even though everything looks the same. And then a sense of trespass comes over me, an uneasy urge to turn around, not wanting to be seen, found out, needing to explain what I am doing here, to apologize for having come this far.

It began here at the Lower Sioux Agency on August 18, 1862. The day before, a small band of young Dakota men stole some food and killed five white settlers in the process. The Dakota feared that white people would seize the opportunity to wipe them out once and for all, and so their chief, Little Crow, agreed to go to war, hoping to drive away the whites.

It is starting to rain as I pull into the parking lot in front of the main building of the museum. I'm the only one in the lot, and I don't see any lights in the window.

In the midst of the Civil War, the government in Washington reneged on payments due by treaty in exchange for land. The Dakota went to ask for food against what was owed to them and were told by the agent that if they were hungry, they should go eat grass or their own dung. The war began with an attack on the agency, where they killed the agent and left him with grass stuffed in his mouth. The fighting raged up and down the Minnesota River, and before it was done more than eight hundred whites and an unknown number of Native Americans were dead. Tens of thousands of terrified settlers fled to the east.

The museum is closed, but the director lets me in. He turns on a few lights in the exhibit area and retreats to his office. The only sound is rain falling on the roof. Around the walls, posters tell of settlement and treaties and the war that finally drove the Dakota away.

I wander the room, stopping before a large photograph of white people huddled together, refugees from the war, staring into the camera, holding one another, fear and exhaustion on their faces, in their eyes, incredulous to have come so far only to go back again.

I go out to the lobby and down the hall to the curator's office, and we talk for a while. He tells me about the territorial commission that set out in 1855 to advertise in the East and in Europe, including Norway, for migrants to come and settle even though there was no land available at the time. This was the idea, to create such a mass of people expecting to find land when they got here that the rest would take care of itself. Which it did, reenacting a pattern that goes all the way back to the original colonists in New England.

It is insidious how white people nibble around the edges to see how much they can get away with, tightening the noose a little more, a little more, until eventually the Native People have had enough. But still the whites keep coming until one day something happens—a few settlers are killed in a dispute—unleashing in whites an urge to annihilate that has been there all along but comes roaring out like the wrath of God in the Old Testament, laying waste to entire villages, killing everyone, the children, slaughtering the animals, burning the corn.

It is a form of terrorism meant to intimidate and disarm—*no matter how you are provoked, if you kill so much as one of us, we will come and kill you all.* It is the same tactic that the Germans used to control most of occupied Europe during World War II.

I go back to the exhibit hall and sit and listen to the rain beating on the roof. To white people, 'to live in peace' was code for doing whatever you wanted without resistance, any sign of which was seen as an act of war, a pretext for extermination and seizure of the land it emptied out. As a result, it was hard to say no when the white man came and offered another of his treaties guaranteeing Native Americans the unmolested safety of land 'farther west' if they would just give up the land they had called their own for longer than they could remember. Whites even offered to pay and promised protection, but, as Thomas Jefferson observed, always with a gun in the other hand, the Godfather putting his arm around your shoulder, the gentle smile, the offer you cannot refuse.

There were almost four hundred such treaties, and *every single one* was broken by white people when it suited them to change their minds, sometimes in a matter of days. They were bound to fail, however sympathetic some whites may have been toward Native American rights. The governor of Georgia expressed the guiding belief of the new country when he said that treaties were no more than "expedients by which ignorant, intractable, and savage people were induced without bloodshed to yield up what civilized people had the right to possess."

In 1869, the U.S. commissioner for Indian Affairs declared that treaties with Native Americans meant nothing, because only nations could enter into treaties and Native American tribes were not nations, because the measure of a nation is the ability to compel its people to honor the terms of a treaty, which is bizarre when you consider that it was the U.S. government that failed again and again to compel its citizens to honor treaties, by which measure the United States was an uncivilized tribe and not to be taken seriously as a sovereign nation.

The curator and I carry on this conversation as if the history were someone else's and not our own. We do not take it to the next level down, do not ask from our hearts what it means for two white men to be having this conversation or what the history has to do with him and me, how we think and feel about ourselves, our ancestors, the place that we call home. We do not look into each other's faces and allow the possibility for some grief and sorrow to pass between us. We play it safe, and the price is a loneliness I will take with me out into the rain.

I say good-bye and thank him for letting me in. He asks where I'm going, why am I here. At the mention of my father and the town of Wells, his face brightens, he being from there, a small world, and then I ask if the Dakota were ever down that far and he nods, oh yes, of course.

The rain has turned into a fine mist as I pull out of the parking lot. The Dakota lost the war, and it was on this ground that the warriors were brought to be tried as criminals, with army officers acting as judge and jury and no one to speak for the defense. Eventually three hundred were sentenced to death after hasty trials, as many as fifty in a single day. President Lincoln later reversed the sentences of all but thirty-eight who were hanged on the day after Christmas, December 26, 1862, in Mankato, Minnesota, the largest mass execution in U.S. history.

Morgan (pop. 903). Most of these towns do not have a restaurant beyond a gas station selling ready-made sandwiches. I turn off the main street by the grain elevators and the railroad tracks and pull in by a cluster of cars and pickup trucks parked in front of what looks to be a place to eat. The interior is like something I imagine out of the 1930s, a high tin ceiling painted powder blue with two slow-moving ceiling fans barely moving the air above large round tables with metal chairs, all of it covered in plastic. To the right is a long counter with a row of stools along the front. Behind is an old black stove and open shelving full of thick white pottery plates and coffee mugs. A handful of elderly people sit at tables and talk quietly among themselves. A lone man behind the counter works the stove, and to judge from the ease he has about him, he must own the place.

I sit on a stool, and he smiles and hands me a well-worn menu.

You're not from here, he says, watching me deciding what to have.

I'm from Connecticut.

So, he says, you came all this way just for me to make you lunch.

That's right, I say, pointing to the grilled chicken sandwich on the menu.

He keeps on talking as he takes a patty of some kind from the freezer and slaps it on the grill. It must be the friendly way he has about him that gets it out of me, about my father being born in Wells and my wanting to see the place now that he has died, might as well, now or never. And then, I just say it, as if it were nothing at all, for the first time since leaving home, about the ashes and trying to find where they belong.

He puts the plate on the counter in front of me.

I guess you'll know it when you find it, he says.

There is something in the tone of his voice, as if what I am out here for is the sort of thing that happens all the time, to all kinds of people, every day, that makes me wonder if it does, if I am searching for something larger than I know.

I find Mankato on the map. The curator at the museum told me about the memorial to the mass execution down by the Minnesota River where it was carried out, Reconciliation Park, on the way to Wells.

My route takes me through New Ulm, named by German settlers after the home they left behind, just as my great-grandparents settled in Iowa in a township called Norway and a village called Thor. When the Germans came for the free land they had been promised, I imagine they had no idea what they were getting into. They would not have understood the hostility from Native People whose land they were about to claim and defend as their own. They would have been in a strange place and frightened, then angry, calling on the army to protect them. Something had been set in motion, which they knew nothing about until it was too late, if at all, that became a juggernaut of greed and hunger and fear and the desperation of longing and hope, and then arrogance and racism and dreams of empire.

The very things that made Europe such a miserable place for so many millions—exploitation, oppression, intolerance, persecution, torture, repression of dissent—were brought across the ocean to be inflicted on Native People who were in the way. As in Europe, a ruling class of landed white men had the most to gain from conquering a continent, but now the lower classes of white people who had been pushed around in Europe had someone they could push around for a change, could feel superior to, entitled to displace and leave destitute and despised and homeless, as many of them had been for generations.

A recipe for disaster if there ever was one.

And then I wonder what would have happened if my great-grandparents had arrived just ten years earlier and had settled in Minnesota instead of Iowa and not been spared what it took to make this land the property of whites, how that would have changed the family stories handed down to me out of which I cannot help but construct some sense of who I am and where and whom I am from.

The highway into Mankato runs south along the western bank of the Minnesota River. I take a bridge across and turn north on a busy divided thoroughfare, two lanes in each direction. In the rush of traffic, I drive right past the memorial and have to turn around. There is a public library and a parking lot beneath a highway overpass.

The memorial is split in two by the busy road. Beside the library is a statue of a Native American elder and a plaque describing "An endeavor to move forward together as one people striving for social change and equality through education and understanding." On the far side of the road is a large statue of a buffalo on the site where the hangings were done in 1862 on a single scaffold, all thirty-eight at once, through the action of a single lever before thousands of troops and cheering crowds.

I cross the street at the light, not wanting to risk the traffic whizzing past.

What does the inscription mean by a 'people' and *which* people are we to move forward together as? I try to imagine what sort of ceremony there was to dedicate the site, the delegation of descendants of the thirty-eight who were hanged together just across the street, how they listened to the white people speak of reconciliation beside the highway overpass, the sound of traffic going by, and what they made of this, and what they make of it now.

Behind the buffalo is a line of trees that almost hides the railroad boxcars sitting on the siding by the river.

Nowhere can I find any mention of what was done here on that day or the reason why or what there is to reconcile or change or understand and what will be done to make it so.

I am beside the road waiting for the light to change, wondering if the people in the cars going by have any idea of where they are or why it matters. What is called for from such a history as the one that brought us here, you in your cars going wherever you are going, me standing here by the side of the road? It has to be more than this, an occasion to be momentarily sad over something we will not bring ourselves to talk about beyond vague expressions of a distant regret.

But are there not things that by their very nature are not meant to be gotten over, because they are not simply in the past?

The road south from Mankato is wet with rain and the wind and big trucks going by knock me around and make me keep a tight hold on the wheel. I glance down at the backpack on the floor and think of the silent little box and that he is never going to tell me what to do with him. He never was. And I cannot escape the sense that there is something more than my father's ashes in there, a presence, a witness, a companion, a guide, I do not know which, maybe all. But for the first time, it is calming to have him there, riding along with me through the rain on our way to the place where he was born.

The road into Wells is lined with American flags on either side, the first such display I have seen in more than a thousand miles. I pass a cemetery thick with small flags and flowers among the tombstones. Even for someone who believes that war is always a bad idea, it is difficult not to be moved by this, so much loss and sacrifice. I turn off the road and park the car and walk up among the graves. What better claim is there to a place than this? But there are none of my relations here. This could be any cemetery in any town except for it being here on what was once the leading edge of the 'westward expansion,' the 'opening' of the West.

There is a painting, *American Progress*, done by John Gast in 1872. Suspended in the air at the center of the frame is the figure of a pale-skinned goddess, a willowy white garment flowing over her body as she floats along, a book held in one hand close to her heart. She is leaning forward with a sense of purpose, leading the way for what is below and behind her, a wagon and a stagecoach and a train and farmers and horsemen and a frame house and oxen pulling a plow, all lit by a bright and sunny sky. And before them, driven by the steady westward progress of Manifest Destiny, is a crowd of Native Americans hunched over in their flight beneath a dark sky along with buffalo and what looks to be a wolf snarling back over its shoulder at the oncoming whites.

I sit beside a tombstone and have my evening smoke. I had not planned to stop, wanting only to get a sense of the town and how to get back here from the hotel in Albert Lea a few miles to the south.

To look around, I would never know whose land this was for thousands of years. When my grandfather came here in 1903 to begin a family, is it possible that he did not know whose land he was living on? How do we see what isn't there and disappeared before we came? What does it leave behind that might tell us where we are?

I get back in the car and drive slowly through the town along tree-lined streets with well-kept houses. Following the map, I cross railroad tracks, which my father mentioned in his memoir, the house being just a block or two away. I wonder if it is still there and will I recognize it from the photographs. It was almost a century ago when my father lived there, and the people, the trees, the house, the front porch may all be gone.

How have I been able for my entire life to keep separate in my mind the history of this country and the story of my family? How it startles me to realize that Gast made his painting in the same year that my great-grandparents got in a horse-drawn wagon and joined the 'westward expansion' to make a life in Iowa. They are right there in the covered wagon leading the way into the 'wilderness.' Did they know who had just been driven into exile over the horizon to make way for them and were being driven still?

I climb into bed and read my book to the sound of rain coming down hard, blowing against the window. I keep reading the same sentence again and again until I close the book and turn out the light to listen to the rain. There is a heaviness gathering inside me, more than fatigue, deeper than sadness, closer to grief. I look across the darkened room at my backpack sitting on a chair, and it comes to me that this grief is not only for my father.

The rain has stopped by the time I wake in the morning. I eat breakfast in the small dining room off the lobby. The news blaring on the television is of a giant crane collapsing in Manhattan, people killed, a terrible thing, and yet I wonder if I need to know about this above everything else I might be thinking of today. Someone left a copy of *USA Today* on the table, and I try not to look.

It is the same everywhere I go, but sameness is not enough to make me feel the presence of something to which I might belong. Sameness and familiarity do not define a People, a common identity that could tell me who I am. Ethnicity is for that, which is not what I am looking at, surface trappings, raw material that does not cohere into something that grabs the soul. Hotels that all look the same, the same fast-food restaurants coast to coast, the same newspaper sitting on the counter in the lobby whether you're in Sioux Falls or Miami Beach—uniformity, a standardization of parts.

I get up and turn off the TV.

I woke this morning thinking of the look on my father's face when he said it did not matter. Perhaps he meant there were many answers to the question and they were all the same to him, of equal value. This is not indifference. That he would or could not choose among the possible answers does not mean the question did not matter. Or the answer was left to me to find. And yet why did he have nothing more to say? Why no curiosity about what the question might have meant to me?

The sky is low and gray and there is a chill in the air even though the forecast is for sun. As I drive north, the land looks like eastern South Dakota, a flat and endless cultivation all around. My father might just as well have been born in the middle of the ocean. Maybe that is what he meant. Anywhere in the ocean is still the ocean, so what does it matter exactly where?

Coming into town I slow the car and say to myself that this is where my father was born, and then I wait to feel something, as if my words might invoke a revelation, but there is just the early-morning traffic and the sun beginning to burn away the clouds.

I drive across the railway tracks and make my way to the address for my grandfather's church. A phone call before I left revealed that it's being converted to a private home. It sits on a corner across from a school, making it easy to find in a town this small. It is brick with a concave roof, and there is no steeple, no stained-glass windows. Near one side is a funeral home. I park in the shade of trees along the street and then get out and walk around, not sure just what I'm expecting to see. Or hoping to.

I keep positioning myself in places and angling the receptors of my soul like a becalmed sailor anticipating a breeze.

There is a dumpster on the lawn and, just beyond, a set of doors. I cup my hands against the glass and peer into the gloom. A child's crib sits on a landing along with pieces of lumber and a bag of concrete. I step back and drop my hands, wondering at the strangeness of the sight, when a young woman's voice from across the street calls out hello with a little rise of uncertainty at the end.

We introduce ourselves and I tell her about my grandfather and she tells me about her friend in northern Minnesota who bought a church to live in, giving her the idea. I ask her what's inside, and she says everything is gone, pews, pulpit, all the trappings of religion. We gutted it, she says.

We say good-bye and I set off on foot to find the house where my father was born. I figure it must have been close by and owned by the church, pastors not having the money to buy one for themselves. I have several pictures of the house, white with a porch running the length of the front, trees on either side. My father is a small boy in the photos, some of which show his mother or his father or an aunt, and, in one, my great-grandfather not too many years before he died, full bearded and smiling into the camera.

I don't know what makes me think I am going to find the house except for a vague belief in magic, deeper and more profound than blind luck, that will reveal it to me in a way so marvelous that I will always remember the exact moment when I realized I was standing before the very house.

I walk down the sidewalk from one island of shade to another, passing two men replacing a roof, high up on a scaffolding, their voices low, speaking Spanish.

When my father was born in 1912, the Dakota War and the mass execution in Mankato were more recent than World War II is today. And the massacre at Wounded Knee was more recent than the Vietnam War is now. This was my father's home, the town where he was born. He was a small boy here, as old when he left for South Dakota as I was when we left Washington for Norway. He must have been born at home. I can't imagine there was a hospital here back then, if there is even one here now.

The neighborhood gives way to a small downtown with a wide concrete roadway, Broadway, which it is, double-width and white in the sun appearing through the clouds. A handful of cars are parked along the street, but almost no one is walking about, the air already stilled by the heat like in mid-July when it's so hot that no one wants to go outdoors.

I go into a pharmacy and ask the woman behind the counter where there is a good place for lunch and she gives me directions to the Wildcat Café. I'm walking down the sidewalk on the shady side of the street when I happen to glance across and see the town hall, which in my town is where they keep the land records. I am halfway across the street when I remind myself that he most likely did not own a house, but I go on anyway, having nothing better to do.

As it turns out, the land records are at the county seat, but I am told I should go downstairs and talk to Zoa.

I find her in a small, windowless office. She is middle-aged and has a kind face and asks me to sit down. I tell her about my grandfather and the church and the house, and she asks if I have a picture. I tell her

I do in the car and hurry out and back to where I parked the car. I'm rifling through the photographs when I see one I had forgotten was there and, when I turn it over, realize it is the house in Hayti where my father lived. I feel a sickening sense of failure, that I went all that way and then forgot I had a photograph and might have been able to find the house, but now it is almost three hundred miles back down the road. I tell myself I might not have found it anyway or maybe it isn't there anymore, but still there is the unmistakable feeling of something lost.

Not that I would have left him there. They lived there only because his father was offered a job, answered the call, which is what charted the course of my grandfather's entire life from one little town and church to another. So it doesn't matter about the photograph, I tell myself walking down the sidewalk, except for this feeling that it's now or never and I am supposed to see it all, not miss a thing, especially when there are so few bits and pieces to go on.

Zoa looks at the photograph and tells me she has seen almost every house in Wells but not this one. She gives me a stack of pictures and says that if I find one of my grandfather's church, I am welcome to have it, but I thank her, no, it's the house I'm looking for. She shakes her head again, sorry not to be any help, and I am just about to go when she rocks forward and pops out of the chair to stride across the room to a large metal cabinet on the wall, muttering that she never takes this out, doesn't want anything to happen to it, and then she has in her hands a pile of newspapers, yellow with age. I stand beside her as she picks up each section with her fingertips, as if she were handling an ancient document that might disintegrate. I clasp my hands behind my back.

She tells me about putting together a centennial edition with a section on churches and now there it is, the last one in the pile. We are shoulder to shoulder, her turning the pages until suddenly she makes a little whoop at the sight of the original Our Savior Lutheran Church, built in 1871, in the middle of a full-page spread.

We're having a good time and still I feel let down, it being the church and not the house.

She pulls back a chair so that I can sit to read. The first part of the article is about the church as a place for keeping alive the culture and community of immigrants, most of whom spoke little English. Services were in Norwegian, and only later did the church begin to offer afternoon services in English.

Reading along I feel a rush at the sight of my grandfather's name in a section on the early pastors, the Rev. J. L. Johnson who came to preach in 1902. There is something about seeing the name that makes the man I never knew more real, that he really lived, that he was here, and then I am past it before I realize what else is there, "who first lived at 365 1st Avenue and later at 491 2nd Street."

"I can't believe it," I say, reading her the line.

"You're kidding," she says. "It says where he lived?"

"I'm getting chills."

She laughs, "So am I."

She knows who lives at those addresses now, which means the houses have not been replaced by a filling station or a parking lot. She is already at her computer, printing out maps to show me the way.

I go to the earlier house first, sure that it's not the one since my father was born ten years after John Lewis came to Wells. And I am right, it bearing no resemblance to the photograph and being too far from the tracks.

The second house is on the other side of town but still no more than a ten-minute walk. A few blocks away I turn a corner and the sight of railroad cars on a siding makes me think of what my mother used to say about rural preachers depending on gifts of food and such and how demeaning it could be. My father never spoke of it to me, but it helps explain why he was so conscious of how much money people had, so easily impressed by the man who had his own airplane or a yacht or a house that was too big for him.

It is the trees I notice first, dwarfing the modest two-story white house on the corner, large enough to be a century old, the trees behind my great-grandfather in the picture with his grandsons.

The front porch is gone, but there is a large gap between the windows on the first and second floors that I take to be the space where the porch roof once attached to the house. At least that is how it seems to me, standing in the street wanting this to be the place where my father was born, somewhere in a bedroom on the second floor.

In the photographs there is no street in front, just a wide lane of grass. In one, my grandfather stands just outside the gate, coming in from his walk home from church on that summer day in 1915. He wears a straw boater and has a smile on his face, looking pleased with himself, his life. All the photographs except the one with my great-grandfather were taken on that same day, which I figured from the date to be a Sunday, the family gathered on this piece of land on the edge of the prairie.

I sit on the grass running down to the curb, half expecting someone to come out of the house and demand to know what I am doing there sitting on their lawn. This is the same ground my father ran across in the picture, just three years old, the same ground on which my grandparents and my great-grandfather stood. I want it to mean something that I can feel in my heart.

The street is quiet, no traffic at this time of day, the town like so many others seeming empty, although there must be people living in these houses. I turn and look again at the house, and as my eye strays down to the foundation, my heart sinks when I see the cinder block, which they did not use a hundred years ago, which means this may not be the house after all. The land but not the house.

A wave of sadness and disappointment comes over me at the thought that this is just another house, anybody's house.

I get up off the curb and walk away.

I am sitting in the car wondering what to do with the rest of the day when it comes to me.

Zoa is with someone when I arrive, and so I wait in the corridor, sitting down, standing up, walking back and forth. The man leaves and she waves me in.

Can you find out if the house is the original? Maybe the foundation was bad and they jacked it up and set it down on a new one. They can do that, can't they?

Zoa takes a book off the shelf behind her desk and finds the page where the property is listed and then picks up the phone and dials and asks the question of someone on the other end. There is a pause, a breathless pause as she waits on the line, the kind of silence where you don't know what is coming but want so much for it to go one way and not the other.

She hangs up the phone. "It was built in 1886," she says and smiles, and I want to cry even though this is such a little thing and yet it opens up a hope I barely knew was there, how much I need for this to be real, an actual house on an actual piece of land where something really happened to form a link in the chain that led to me.

We sit for a while, Zoa and I, talking about families and lineage and the town. I recall what the curator said about this once being Dakota land and ask her about the controversy I read about online when I was educating myself about the Dakota War of 1862. Minnesota is about to celebrate its 150th anniversary as a state, and members of the Dakota nation are protesting a lack of recognition of what was done to them in order to bring that history about. She says she hasn't heard of it but goes on to talk about her own ancestry, which is Sami, also known as Lapp, and how she once was shocked to hear someone describe the Sami as the 'niggers of Norway,' long ago driven to the far north by the people who now call themselves Norwegians.

When I say good-bye to Zoa, I thank her for being so kind, and she looks into my eyes and says, "I'm glad you came to Wells and found kindness."

On my way out of town, I go back to the house and take some photographs. I stop at the cemetery and sit on the grass in the shade of a tree and let the tears come in. Then I take my father and myself back to the hotel.

Sleep comes hard and when it does, not for long. For days I have been waiting for the land to speak to me, to answer the riddle, but either I cannot hear or it has nothing to say. At least to me.

Why does it matter who we are in relation to the land? And how am I to know?

A quarter past eleven, I'm lying in the dark, staring up at the ceiling.

When Native Americans ask for the return of their land, what exactly are they asking for? And when the government says no, what is it refusing to give up? And are they the same?

I think Native Americans are asking for the return of the place where they are from, that tells them who they are and where they are meant to return. A sacred place, more than itself, not simply the place where they were born. I was born in Washington, D.C., my brother and sister in California, my father in Minnesota, my mother in Wisconsin—none of which tells you who we are or where we truly belong, the place that if it were taken from us, we could not rest until we had it back. These are just locations on a map. They could be more—if they were sacred to us, holy, defining, land as self, to embody the Divine—if we related to the land in that way. But we do not.

Native Americans do and always have, which is why they want it back.

And we, the people of the United States, say no. And why?

I doubt there is for us a square yard of truly sacred ground on the entire continent, so whatever it is we are hanging on to, it isn't that.

It is the story we keep telling ourselves to keep from having to admit how wrong it was, centuries of illusion and denial slipping away to reveal the arrogance, the greed, the pathetic need to think ourselves superior, what James Baldwin meant about feeling sorry for white people, having to depend on thinking they are better than everyone else.

If the Lakota are right about the Black Hills belonging to them, what else are they right about? And who among us wants to know?

Just past 1:00 A.M., I wake from a dream I can almost remember but then watch it disappear in the darkness above my face.

If I were from a place, if that were true, then I imagine it would feel something like a plant or a tree growing from the ground. It would be in my body, a state of mind, a condition of my soul. I say these things with certainty because that is how it comes to me even though I have no idea of what it is to feel that way about any place on earth. Like so many others, my ancestors came in search of land mostly as a thing to be owned and exploited and changed into something else so they might make a living and accumulate money and possessions and still more land. That they would eventually be buried here seems almost incidental, 'here' simply being where they were when they happened to die.

However much they may have loved to walk upon the land, the view from the ridge or the valley floor, the feel of the soil in their hands, there is nothing I can see to suggest that it was sacred to them. If it were, they would not be so quick to pack up and leave if they could find something a little better farther on. This whole country was built on that singular idea, the restless impulse to move on to something and somewhere else, better pickings, an opportunity, getting there first, the promise of more, everything a means to some end other than itself.

My ancestors were not among the settlers who came to Jamestown in search of gold and silver, believing that North America would do for England what the land to the south had done for Spain and make them and their masters more rich and powerful than they already were. But even the Pilgrims who came in search of religious freedom also came for land to own and prosper on and to provide a return on investment to their backers in England.

In the first two hundred years of settlement, many of the white people who came were convicts and rebels and the homeless and children snatched off the streets of London and Liverpool, and Scots and Irish driven off their land to make way for English and Scottish Protestants. They were bound in various forms of servitude and slavery to the wealthy and propertied class, and most never got the piece of land they were promised in return. So the habit of making promises never to be kept goes back all the way to the beginning.

And then there were the Africans brought here in chains, who were stolen by white people *from* their land and to whom no promises were made to then be broken.

I make some oatmeal and eat it sitting up in bed with the lights turned off. The air is still and quiet except for the sound of the spoon scraping the plastic bowl and my mouth working the food.

Were my ancestors the owners or the owned? Or both?

I go back beneath the covers and try to sleep.

I wake at 5:25 A.M., groggy, tired, a long day ahead, first to Decorah, Iowa, and the Norwegian-American Museum, and then almost two hundred miles more to Thor and Fort Dodge.

I wish I could remember my dreams.

I take a shower to wake myself up. There is no hurry to pack, since the museum does not open until 9:00 and it's only a few hours away.

When we visited Hardanger fifteen years ago, I remember someone saying as we drove along looking at the mountains and the water, who would leave such a place who did not have to? And when you do leave such a place, does it make a wound, and does it end with you? Is that what I felt in my heart, the sadness of having to leave a place I had never been?

The breakfast room is noisy with a family on vacation. I find a table by the window in the corner.

I think I do not remember my dreams because since leaving home, I am in something like a dream state all the time.

I go upstairs and finish packing and then call Heather, my second cousin once removed, who lives in Fort Dodge and until a few years ago owned the house where my great-grandparents made a life for themselves and their six children. I am startled to hear that she already knows my name, has seen pictures of me through my cousins Bill and Jim, and knows about my father and Geraldine. And yet I had never heard of her or any of her relations until a few weeks ago. My father never told me because I did not ask, but he also never took it upon himself to tell me on his own. Was his rootlessness the cause, what made him think I did not need to know, one more thing that made no difference?

I am driving east along the interstate, which I have avoided until now, when the opening bars of "Amazing Grace" come into my mind, and I begin to sing. I keep it up for quite a while.

Turning south toward Iowa, it occurs to me that white people could have left vast tracts of land to Native Americans—half a continent—and still have had a prosperous nation. But we were determined to have it all, to build an empire. We would have taken Canada if we could have gotten away with it. And there were those in favor of claiming all of Mexico instead of just the half we took after provoking a war for the sole purpose of seizing more land. After that, the only thing in our way was the Pacific Ocean, which did not keep us from taking Hawaii and then the Philippines as a gateway to Asian markets, which it would have been if Filipinos had not put up such a fight, if their belief in their own right to freedom and self-determination had not been so stubborn.

Why do I keep saying 'we'? I had no hand in this history. I wasn't even alive. So who is this 'we' I keep speaking of? Why do I feel the need to include myself?

Because everyone needs a 'we,' and it's the only one I've got?

I cross the border into Iowa and see a sign for Decorah, where my father and his brother attended Luther College and where I was invited to speak several years ago.

Maybe what I have to do is what my father was really telling me that day without either of us knowing it, that I have to find a way to make it matter.

Slowing to pass through a small town, I see a horse and buggy parked outside a store, and then out comes a man with a dark beard and a straw hat, and a child beside him, holding his hand, and I realize they must be Amish, whom I had not expected to see so far west. I glance into the mirror to see them getting into the buggy and setting off. My great-grandparents would have come across Illinois and into Iowa in a wagon drawn by horses. I wonder if they were alone or with others in a caravan, what they imagined about the place they were going to and the life they would live, and were they afraid.

The Norwegian-American Museum, also called *Vesterheim* for 'western home,' recalls the Norwegian immigrant experience during the nineteenth century. I stand in the cool, airy lobby and feel the stillness of the place, there being just me and a young woman behind the counter. She smiles and says good morning.

This must have been an old factory building, the wide floorboards creaking beneath my feet. The first exhibit is a reproduction of a rustic house in Telemark, a county in the southeastern part of Norway not too far from Oslo, where we lived when I was a boy. There are reds and pale blues—they liked to paint the furniture—a loom, a long table, enclosed beds against the wall, and suddenly there are tears coming into my eyes as if I am remembering something I left behind a long time ago, and yet I have never been to such a place as I am standing in now, so what is there to miss? I close my eyes and smell the wood and all the rest that I cannot name, wondering what sort of memory is this, strange in my mind and yet so familiar to the rest of me.

Only Ireland lost a greater percentage of its population through emigration to the United States. Beginning in the 1820s, Norwegians came mostly from farms and fishing villages, driven by economic hardship, farms being subdivided through primogeniture, not enough jobs in the cities, a rigid class system, a state-dominated church.

I am in a room full of wooden objects—furniture, bowls, trunks, dishes—all hand-carved and brightly painted in reds and blues. I sit down on a bench against the wall.

When emigrants left Norway, they went as Norwegians. If you start off knowing who you are, then you can go anywhere, live anywhere, even for the rest of your life, and with your dying breath still know who you are. And if you live in an isolated town on the prairie, the same can be true of your children. I have no doubt that my grandfather, growing up speaking Norwegian at home and in church and his community, thought of himself as Norwegian even as he counted himself a newly minted American. As did my father. But the hand-off failed when it came to me. The artifacts in this room are familiar, but in no way are they mine.

What if you do not start out knowing who you are? Or start out thinking you are one thing that turns out to be another? There is no 'American ethnicity.' There is no defining body of culture, of music, dance and costume, literature, story and myth, of food and custom and ritual, that resonates in the hearts of all who call themselves American simply because they *are* American, that tells them who they are as one People from a single place. We do have our moments, but they are few and far between, and so we try to compensate by making *that*—our non-ethnicity, our diversity, the fictitious melting pot—into what is missing. But it's not the same.

There being no American ethnicity makes it relatively easy for a Norwegian to become accepted as American but much harder the other way around. There is nothing I could do that would make me Norwegian.

So if my father did not raise me to think of myself as Norwegian as his father did for him, then it was only a matter of time before I discovered that I have no ethnicity at all. I am a citizen of a nation-state, a political, economic, legal, and civic fact, but I am not ethnic. The people of the United States are not my People in the sense that my father would have regarded any gathering of Norwegians anywhere in the world as in some way his own.

I have no People, as if I came from nowhere and nowhere is where I am. And yet this is where I was born, the only home I have ever known. I am a walking displacement of soul.

In the lobby I wander into a gift shop full of books and knickknacks, brightly costumed dolls, a few from Hardanger, and wonder if my great-grandmother had one of these and did she leave it behind. There is clothing and postcards and painted dishes, lefse pans, all of it familiar and strange.

A displacement in time, a displacement in space coming together inside me, catching up across the generations, coalescing, cohering into grief.

In a little restaurant next door, I find a table in the corner and order lunch, asking for a piece of lefse with my soup. I remember from Norway the thin potato pancake with many uses. It was great for wrapping up a hotdog.

They come from Norway and create a little Norway in the middle of Iowa. They call it Norway Township and the tiny village Thor, after the Norse god of Thunder, provider of protection, last pagan holdout against the encroachment of Christianity. They play at being American only as much as it takes to be left alone and undisturbed. They know that anyone making a show of being from somewhere else risks being ostracized, made fun of, singled out. Germans, Norwegians, Irish, Scots, Swedes, Dutch—all have their enclaves with newspapers in their native tongues that they read as they teach themselves enough English to get along.

Lunch arrives, a bite of lefse, just as I remember it. I ask for another piece, with butter and sugar to sprinkle on top.

Sooner or later, of course, they must become American, not so much by turning into something new as by giving something up. They become American by ceasing to be Norwegian, by blending in, by entering a negative space defined by what it is not. They try to lose the accents and the clothes and change their names to prove their sincerity by abandoning part of who they are.

They also cannot fail to notice what happens to anyone not considered white—black people most of all, but also Irish, Mexicans, Greeks, Jews, Asians, Native Americans, Slavs—and so take care to make being white a part of who they are seen to be. As James Baldwin put it, the Norwegian farmer was not white until he came to the United States, just as the African was not black.

The English, of course, are above such things, being the ones in charge, God's chosen people who own most of the land and run the politics and the banks. They bring with them an abiding belief in their own superiority over anyone who is not English and the authority to decide what it means to be American and white.

Everyone is supposed to speak English, the language of England, even though the vast majority are not from there. Not even the English are really English anymore. I am no more that than I am Norwegian. I am an American working to forget whatever might remind me that I am really from somewhere else, that this is not who I am, and if it is, it is only because something has been lost that I try not to see, because the emptiness, the awareness of the gaping hole where it is supposed to be would be too hard to bear. I work to make it disappear, the remnant, the reminders of who and what I came from generations ago. It becomes a *goal*, this forgetting, this blotting out. And from the wake closing in behind comes an emptiness rooted in such a distant past that I may have no idea what it is.

Except when I bite down on the lefse and turn away so no one will see my eyes.

The road from Decorah winds south through rolling green hills, a welcome change from prairie, if only for a while.

Lineage is not what I am from. Lineage is what connects me to it, a map, a trail of crumbs that cannot by itself take me anywhere. Nor can it make me feel that I belong once I arrive, that anyone will recognize my name or my face or feel obliged to take me in. And sometimes the map points to a destination that is no longer there.

Before Europeans arrived, it was not uncommon for Native Americans to migrate vast distances across North America, sometimes thousands of miles over many years. But when they moved, they went as bands and communities, as a People, sometimes an entire nation, leaving nothing behind and always taking with them a deep identification with the land and all things. The Algonquin Nation in the Northeast was still the Algonquin Nation in the Midwest, physically and spiritually intact.

But when my great-grandparents left Norway, or my more distant relations departed England, they crossed an ocean that would separate them from not only pieces of geography but also tribes that had anchored their existence by providing a sense of origination and belonging. They displaced themselves in the pursuit of opportunity, willing to give up their past in exchange for the promise of a better life, while many others came because they were compelled, pushed out by war and persecution and poverty and governments wanting to be rid of them and capitalists eager to make use of them for the lowest possible price.

They had burned their bridges, which was hard enough without the fact that indigenous Peoples had already been living here for tens of thousands of years. But the English in particular were never known for their ability to share. And so Native Peoples had to be got rid of if the displaced Europeans were ever going to feel they had a home among people they considered their own in a country that was theirs.

The road turns west at Calmar, and the land begins to flatten out again.

In 1871, Nils bought land in Thor and put in a first crop, while in Washington, D.C., Congress passed a law ending the practice of making treaties with Native Americans. From then on, the United States could do whatever it wanted, because Native Americans were no longer recognized as nations to be negotiated with. And in 1874, an army led by George Armstrong Custer, Long Hair, *Pehin Hanska*, invaded the Black Hills in search of gold, which they found "from the grass roots down," marking the beginning of the end for the Plains Nations.

These pairings never came up for me before because I never knew the story of my family well enough—dates and places and faces and the choices that make a life—to align it with a larger history. And the closer I get to Thor, the more frequent those linkages become, and their accumulated weight presses my resistance to knowing what all of this has to do with me and what I have come to do.

At New Hampton I am back on the Great Plains, big sky dotted with white clouds, a beautiful day, at last.

My great-grandparents could not have bought the acres in Thor if other white people had not first stolen them by force or fraud, which makes it fair to say they were in receipt of stolen property. As I understand the law, you are not allowed to keep such a thing no matter how innocent you are of the original theft. Unless you have the power to decide what is stolen and what is not, which my great-grandparents did not have themselves but were counted among those who did.

And if I go further back on my mother's side, back to the seventeenth century, when Native Americans were hunted and massacred throughout southern New England, then it is more than a matter of being in receipt of property stolen by someone else. I would like to think that my Griswold, Bailey, and Dudley ancestors had no part in the drive to remove and exterminate, but I have to assume that at least some of them did. A few may even have stood against it, but, still, this is what was done by enough and with the tacit consent of all the rest, and because of it there was land and water and the makings of the most prosperous nation the world has ever seen.

I have done nothing wrong myself, and yet I know this story is connected to my own. My life is a thread embedded in a web of relation, and the farther down this road I go, the closer I come to Thor, where my great-grandparents lived and died and are buried on the land, the more I feel the presence of the past. I am guilty of nothing, I have nothing to be ashamed of, and yet guilt and shame are woven into the fabric that holds my life.

I cannot see by what special right I would get to choose which threads to own and which to disavow, as if they have nothing to do with me. There are no threads, only the web, whole and entire with all its stories, the ones that make me proud and the ones that break my heart and make me want to turn away. I sometimes act as if it is possible to stand alone, disconnected, autonomous, accountable only to myself, making up my life as I go along, no one's story but my own, but it's not.

A sign reads "Charles City: America's Hometown," an advertisement for a place to call home, where you could be from if only you were willing to pick up and move from where you are. The scenery is pretty and the people are friendly and there are jobs, and in America you can go anywhere and call it home, a useful trait for refugees and wanderers, for explorers, for colonizers and conquerors.

I think of my father and his ability to adopt each new post in his reenactment of the immigrant experience. He was a perpetual immigrant, a career displaced person who could fit in almost anywhere, any culture, any other People's land, or any president's foreign policy. And belong nowhere. He was a third-generation American and yet still a displaced Norwegian somewhere inside himself. And, so quick to add, also American.

We are a nation of hyphenated displaced also's.

Will the real Valdemar please stand up? Will the real American?

It comes upon me with no warning at all, the ordinary sign by the side of the road with the arrow pointing straight ahead to Dakota City, eight miles, and then the one below pointing left and south to Thor just three miles away. I stop the car on the gravel shoulder and get out and lean against the door as I gaze down County Road P-66, the land looking as it has for the last 1,500 miles and yet, for me, suddenly not the same at all.

I have been waiting all this time to feel something at just this moment, about to turn down the road that will take me into Thor, Iowa, all this way to look out on this particular expanse of plowed earth, and yet what I feel is tired and a little foolish.

I looked up the address of the farm on the Internet and got the satellite view, so I know where I am going. The village of Thor appears like so many tiny midwestern towns. It has a run-down feeling as if they pour everything into the land with not much left over for anything else, no stores or gas stations, only a few houses on the handful of short streets branching out to either side. The Lutheran church, of course, is well maintained. I am barely past it when I am out the other side of town going south, plowed fields all around, knowing that I am near, a few miles down the road, and then turning left on 270th Street—they number everything out here, like taking inventory—my eyes filling up and then I am squinting to make out the number on the mailbox and I think it is the one but no, it's not, and then there it is, so sudden and beautiful, the front yard shaded by a grove of tall trees that my great-grandparents must have planted, and I am crying now, driving past, pulling over so I don't go off the road into a ditch.

An adopted child who one day comes upon the parents' graves is both moved and disappointed to be so close and yet to know it can never be what is needed, cannot fill in what is missing.

I turn around and drive past the house and then turn south toward Fort Dodge. I start to cry, stop the car, start up again, begin to cry. It is just a house on a plot of land, a two-story white clapboard farmhouse with trees out front. I have never met the people who live there now or anyone who lived there before. It is only a house.

There is barely any shade out on the prairie. I pull off the road and get out of the car and lean against the hood to have my evening smoke. Better here than the parking lot of a Super 8. The wind is strong and hot at my back. I am quiet, waiting for whatever is coming now.

I make my supper and take a shower and climb into bed. *Spider-Man* is playing on the TV. I want to be anywhere but here. I am already disappointed by the feeling that I will go home unchanged except for being without my father's ashes. I sat with him as he died and am trying to do right by him again. Unless it really doesn't matter

> maybe this is all for nothing and
> either way I will be unchanged or changed but not enough
> *let yourself dissolve and you will know who you are*
> okay, okay

I shut off the TV and turn out the light and lie in the dark to the sound of traffic on the road running by the hotel. Tomorrow is Sunday and I will go to church and meet three more of my cousins and hear stories of my relations. I called the pastor, Chris, before I left home, and she said they celebrated an anniversary not long ago and there is a basement full of documents and photographs I can look at if I want. It was then that she invited me to attend a service—two, in fact, the 9:00 A.M. in Eagle Grove, where my cousins Loretta and Jim live, and then the 10:30 service in Thor. I told her I have never been to a Lutheran church, but she said not to worry and who knows, maybe they would make a believer out of me, and then she laughed.

In Minneapolis, when I heard Bill and Jim speak of 'Grandpa' and 'Great-grandpa' with the ease of naming the ordinary and familiar, I felt such a pain of envy that they could so casually do what I have never been able to, has never occurred to me as even possible. I say the words out loud, softly, trying them out, but they seem strange and disembodied, unreal.

Immigrant grief is knowing you can never be home again in the way you were. Nils and Margret could have gone back to Norway and been Norwegian there, and perhaps their children could have done the same. But with each generation, the ability to go back becomes less and less until it disappears. So the grief of immigrants need not be their own, but their children's and their children's children's, born into a strange land without the benefit of knowing just how strange it is and how far they really are from home, yet all the while told that is exactly where they are.

There is no place on earth where I can feel the way I imagine Nils Måkestad felt in Hardanger or the way almost everyone on the planet can feel about the place where they live, because it is also where they are from, where the language of their ancestors is heard every day and in their dreams at night.

All across the United States, Native Americans are working to reclaim and preserve what the rest of us have long since lost or are rushing headlong to forget in the name of being counted as American.

And how ironic it is that we keep going around the world proclaiming who we are, champions of 'freedom' and 'democracy,' even at the barrel of a gun, and presuming that our version of those ideas is the only one there is, as if 'democracy' as practiced in the United States is what democracy *is.*

If we really are superior, why this need to keep pointing it out, to trumpet 'American values' and 'the American way of life,' which my father made his career, to work at it so hard, as if it were a matter of life and death that everyone should know? When all the while, the problem is not that they do not know who we are. It is that *we* do not.

I brought along a pair of slacks to look nice when I go to church to meet my relations. Chris assured me they were very casual, although some older members might wear suits and ties. I do not want them to think I lack respect, and since I never go to church, I am conscious of being a guest and not wanting to offend. Before going down for breakfast, I clean my shoes.

My father could have taken any phone book in Norway and picked out a hundred names at random and felt some kinship with them all. That is simply not possible in a nation of immigrants, where everyone is ultimately from a different somewhere else. Perhaps the best that I can do is leave my father's ashes in a township called Norway in a town called Thor, in a small gathering of Norwegian bones in the middle of the vast North American prairie.

After breakfast I pack my bags and sit on the bed, not wanting to go. I am shy, even scared of these people I do not know and their religion. I am an outsider, even though I know they will be gracious and polite, but to a visitor, a temporary guest, not someone who belongs, who would be missed.

Then again I could be wrong, I think, wheeling my suitcase through the door and down the hall. I have never been here before. I do not know what will happen.

I am to meet my cousin Loretta and her brother Jim at the Lutheran church in Eagle Grove. Then I will go a few miles to the west to attend a second service at the church in Thor. Loretta and Jim are my second cousins, a term I never understood until now because I had no reason to. That came as a surprise to me, but not as much as when I told other people of my discovery, a little embarrassed coming into it so late, only to find that not one person knew it for themselves, putting me in the strange position of being the one to pass it on. What does it mean to live in a place where the difference between a first and second cousin—the most basic nomenclature of lineage and relation—is something people routinely do not know?

I practice to make the strange familiar. First cousins share the same grandparents, as I do with Bill and Jim in Minnesota. Second cousins have only great-grandparents in common. Loretta and Jim are the grandchildren of my grandfather's sister, Margaret (named for her mother), so our grandparents are not the same. But our great-grandparents—the parents of our grandparents—we have in common. My cousin Heather down in Fort Dodge, whom I will meet tonight, is my second cousin, once removed, being the child—one generation removed—of another of my second cousins, who is a grandchild of my grandfather's older brother, Lars. Saying all of this out loud makes people shake their heads and smile, too much to grasp. And yet already I can feel exactly what it means and the significance of it that has so quickly lodged itself in my heart. I have relations and a language that not so much locates me in some precise way—which is impossible in a web that is constantly changing—but that makes me aware that the web exists and always has. And in learning to name who we are in relation to one another, I am moved not so much by the people or the names but by the realization of how far removed my life has been from feeling that I am anyone from anyplace at all.

I drive past the farmhouse on the way to Eagle Grove, slowing down, noticing the early-morning shadows cast by trees in front of the house, the soft morning light over the fields.

The church and town are larger and more prosperous than I expected after seeing so many sad, disappearing towns. I park the car and go inside, willing myself to look people in the eye so they will say good morning and I will feel less strange. In the vestibule I stand somewhat awkwardly until Chris intuits that I must be me by the way I'm looking around, wanting to be found, and she comes over and introduces herself, and suddenly everything is okay. We sit on a bench and wait for Loretta and pass the time in idle talk about my trip, which I explain to her in the usual way, my father dying, wanting to meet my relations. She glances at her watch and then excuses herself to go prepare for the service.

I go inside and take a seat in a pew at the back, thinking Loretta and Jim still might show up.

This is my first time at a Lutheran service and I bring to the experience only what I know of Martin Luther tacking up his theses on the door, and his virulent anti-Semitism. And then, of course, there is Garrison Keillor on *Prairie Home Companion*, who never passes up an opportunity to make fun of Lutherans, if always with affection. But the service seems to my untrained eyes and ears much the same as others that I've seen, the scripture, the singing, the homily. The singing always makes me want to cry, not the words or the music, but the voices joined together. And then toward the end a young man gets up to sing on his own, nervous, earnest, touching me more deeply than all the rest.

When it's over, I say good-bye to Chris, who says my cousins may have got their signals crossed and will probably be waiting for me in Thor: "They know you're coming."

And they do. After the service in Thor, I am approached by someone who startles me by knowing who I am and then directs me downstairs, "where the Lothe family is expecting you." My grandfather's sister Margaret married Dan Lothe, who is famous in my imagination as the towering figure of Uncle Dan whose farm my brother and sister visited when I was just a baby and was left behind in Washington with my mother.

There is a brass plaque on the wall listing the names of members of the church who have been ordained as pastors, my grandfather at the top. I pause, puzzled to see 'Johan' instead of 'John,' but then I am being led through a door and down the stairs into a large activity room with folding tables and metal chairs and a small group of people waiting just for me. I feel shy as I put out my hand to Loretta, who squints and smiles as she gestures toward her brother Jim and her husband, Ron, and a man called Roger, who is no relation but introduces himself as not the oldest one in the room but the one with the best memory. Everyone laughs in a way that says they've heard it many times before.

We settle in around the table, Loretta arranging a small pile of books and papers in front of her, making a little shrug, casting about for a place to begin. And then, how easily we seem to put ourselves in motion, off and running for more than an hour of animated talk about family and who's related to whom, with one book tracing our line back in Norway to 30 B.C. How is that possible, I wonder? Is it? And how does it matter?

The genealogy lists my sister and my brother, but there is no mention of me. I understand, and yet it is strange not to find myself in the story where I'm supposed to be.

"Our great-grandpa," says Loretta, telling a story, which I don't really hear at first, the 'our' filling up my mind, 'our' as in Loretta's and Jim's and mine, our great-grandpa, one and the same, which seems a kind of miracle.

She tells of Nils arriving in 1871 to buy land and plant a crop, building a sod house, harvesting the crop, and then going back to Illinois for Margret.

Loretta has made photocopies of documents that she hands to me as we stand and get ready to go, just where I'm not sure, having no idea what if anything comes after this. I am totally prepared for them to say good-bye, shake my hand, say how glad they were to meet me. But Loretta has a plan, which she follows with no need to comment, as if I already knew or should have known, that of course we are going to see the family cemetery, and then we'll all go over to Jim's house, which sits on land that was once part of the original farm, and we will sit around the dining-room table and say a prayer and share a Sunday dinner together.

It is the fact that all of this was taken for granted by everyone but me, anything else being unthinkable, absurd, that moves me in ways I find hard to express.

A mile or two down the county highway south of Thor, there is a dirt road running off to the left, surfaced in white stone with a center strip of grass. It leads to a tiny island of green in the middle of a one-square-mile section of field. It is the West Ullensvang Cemetery, I am told, there being no sign. We park the cars on the grass. The cemetery is perhaps fifty feet square in all, with just a few dozen graves. There is a large spruce in the middle providing shade, surrounded by a scattering of smaller trees. Loretta points out that the spruce was planted by Nils after the death of his wife, our great-grandmother.

What kind of spruce, I ask.

Black Hills.

The air is still and quiet but for birds in the fields, singing.

A large granite stone in the middle reads:

N. M. Johnson 1839–1924
Margret, his wife 1842–1908

and a smaller stone on the right is for my great-uncle Dan and my great-aunt Margaret.

I think of my father's ashes sitting in my backpack in the car over there on the grass. Loretta is naming some of the people buried here, including Ole W. Willickson from Hardanger, the first settler to come to Thor. And then she's talking of someone scattering ashes a short while ago—not sure, a rumor—and I wonder aloud, trying to sound casual, how one gets permission, if it's required. She doesn't know, probably the township, the ones who keep up the cemetery. I nod and walk away, looking down at the stones, trying not to let on that I care.

Cousin Jim lives in a house on the western edge of what was once the Johnson farm, built when a parcel was sold to the eldest son almost a hundred years ago. In back is a beautiful hip-roofed barn that looks tired and wanting to lie down. When I get out of the car, a huge yellow Lab comes bounding over and wants in the worst way to jump up on me, but I know enough about dogs to keep him off as Jim recounts how he rescued him from the pound and hasn't taught him manners yet.

We go inside and Loretta busies herself with dinner, regretting the salad she forgot in her refrigerator at home. Then it's time to eat, and we all sit around the dining-room table and someone says grace, and although I do not share in their religion, there is no boundary around grace and giving thanks, and this place seems full of both.

There is chicken from the grill and scalloped potatoes and asparagus from Loretta's garden and then strawberry pie for dessert. I cannot remember the last time I had a piece of pie.

The talk turns to farming and the land, about which there are strong opinions. The Johnson farm has been sold except for the houses and the land on which they sit. The price of farmland has gone so high that speculators and corporations are moving in, making offers people find themselves unable to refuse, especially when they're getting old and thinking to retire, as many of them are, with their children moving off the land for opportunities away from the farm.

Farmers are cutting down trees so they can plant the corn road-to-road. There was a time not long ago when you could not look out across the prairie and see neighboring towns because the trees were in the way, but now you can.

But, I ask, don't the trees slow the wind and keep the topsoil in place so you don't have another dust bowl, like in the Great Depression?

Nods around the table, well, of course.

But then why cut them down?

They say farmer friends roll their eyes at the idea of hanging on to a bunch of trees when there is big money to be made by cutting them down and planting corn that gets turned into ethanol.

The rivers have lost their fish, such that you can eat, because of run-off from the pig farms, which is also doing things to the drinking water. And there are fewer people around because the machines have gotten so big that you don't need so many hands anymore. They used to have tillers that did a few rows at a time, but the new ones can turn over twenty or thirty in a single pass. Of course there's no point to having a machine that big unless you have a monster piece of land to run it on, so the big farms keep getting bigger by driving out the smaller ones that can't compete.

White people are driving white people off the land. It is nothing new, getting rid of 'surplus population,' whether from the slums of England or New York, driving people westward with promises of something better to replace what the elites have made unlivable. Except now the western frontier is gone.

We say good-bye and Loretta walks me to the car. I tell her I am hoping to see inside the original house while I'm here and she says she would like to see it, too, and how about tomorrow, and I'm surprised to hear her say it, that we should have this need in common, with her living so close by.

I tell her I will talk with Heather, who knows the people living there now, and let her know.

I stop at the cemetery on my way to Fort Dodge. I feel like a thief casing a heist, figuring how to come in unobserved, how to conceal what I am doing, how to get safely away. I feel foolish to be feeling this way, but I do not want to ask permission because the answer might be no. I have come too far to take the chance. And I cannot spread the ashes on the farm, not on speculated, corporate ground, and Loretta said it's only a matter of time before the houses are torn down to extend the fields to grow more corn to make more money for someone who lives somewhere else.

I asked her how long she thought the cemetery would last. "Oh, forever."

Theft is not the crime. It is trespass, a feeling I have had almost from the start, of not having the right to be here. It is true that I am here and no one is telling me to leave, but that doesn't mean it is by right, only that the moment of being sent away hasn't yet arrived. I am related by blood to several of those long buried in this ground, as is my father, and yet even that is not enough to make this feeling go away. But it will have to be, because I have no other place to go and I have decided it will be here because it feels as close to right as it will ever be.

I sit on the grass beside Nils and Margret and introduce myself, I am Allan, your great-grandson—tears coming in at the sound of my voice speaking the words—my father died and I have brought his ashes here. They are over there in the car. He told me it didn't matter where they went, but it does to me and you never know, it just might to him after all, and so I thought I should come and see.

Heather is in her thirties, young and full of life. It is late in the afternoon when she meets me in Fort Dodge. She has the night shift and got out of bed just a little while ago and hasn't long before she goes back to work. She is driving me to her house—there are some things she wants me to see—and we talk about night shifts and the farm and how hard it was for her to sell the house when the commute got to be too much.

She shows me the painted plates her grandmother did, proudly displayed. I lean in close—they are beautiful—and I do the figuring in my mind, *by the daughter of my grandfather's older brother.* I need to do this, a kind of mapping that keeps me oriented in a relational space that has been more populated over the last seven days than in the previous sixty years. She shows me around the house. How odd it seems, the two of us here, complete strangers and yet in some way intimates of a sort I know little about. It's like being in church for the first time in years and not knowing the hymns and trying to catch the tune because I feel foolish just standing there staring down at the hymnal and it does feel good to hear my voice blending in with all the rest.

On the wall is a photograph of Nils and Margret and their six children, a formal pose, looking very serious in their Sunday clothes. There is Lars and Martin and Mandius and my grandfather, John—or was it still Johan then?—and standing on the left is Loretta's grandmother, Margaret, and seated in the front are the parents, with Margret looking rather stern with her hair so flat against the top of her head that it makes me wonder how tight the bun must be in back, and Nils with his full beard and soft eyes that gaze into the middle distance. Between them is Selma, the youngest, who has such a look on her face that it startles me, not so much for her beauty, which is considerable, as for the sense of purpose and resolve, looking not simply into the camera but as if she knows just whom she's looking at and wants certain things to be absolutely clear, the most important of which is that she intends to have a life that is her own, like the young woman in *My Brilliant Career*.

I hold out the picture to Heather and point to Selma and tell her what I see, and she nods and says, oh, yes, that Selma was a real character who traveled and spent most of her life unmarried.

I tell her I would like to have a copy, and she gets some tools to remove it from the frame. We drive to Walmart, where the man behind the counter refuses to make a copy because the original was done by a professional photographer—you can tell just by looking at it, he says—and there are copyright issues. I stand there staring down at the photograph, my mind slowly catching up to the idea that someone could actually get sued over this. It was more than a hundred years ago, I say, and it is our family, thinking surely that will do the trick but no, shaking his head and saying he's sorry, it's a rule.

Heather says she knows a way and we drive to a supermarket where they have a scanner and we make the copies, one each for her and me and Loretta. We joke about the life of crime we have embarked upon, a bonding experience. It's getting late and she is due at work, so she takes me back to the hotel. We say good-bye and I thank her and tell her I will send a photo of Nils that she may not have seen that was my father's, and as she waves and drives away, it occurs to me that I will probably never see her again.

I get in my car and drive to Humboldt, a few miles to the north, where I will stay for the rest of my time here, it being closer to Thor and the county courthouse where the land records are kept.

Monday morning, my eighth day, waking to clouds out the window and the sound of rain, I lie in bed and think about Roger in the church yesterday, talking about his belonging to the Sons of Norway, a fraternal organization for preserving the language and customs and assisting those in need. The Johnsons spoke Norwegian at home for two generations, which I imagine would be impossible today. I asked Loretta the same question I put to my father about considering himself Norwegian, and she said she called herself Norwegian American until she finally gave in to her kids telling her to stop. They had no way of knowing what they were asking her to do, since they never had what she was giving up.

When we came back from Norway and lived in Massachusetts, there was a Polish man who came to collect our garbage, which he fed to his pigs. My father spoke fluent Polish and was home on leave from Warsaw when he happened to meet the man outside the house as he was making his collection, and because my mother had told him about the man, my father greeted him in Polish. The man began to cry.

I wonder if my father was able to hang on to his identity as Norwegian because he spent so much of his life outside the United States in countries that did not require that he conceal who he was. And then he could come 'home' on leave and visit his family or serve a stint in Washington before going on to the next assignment overseas. Was he passing as an American all that time? We used to joke that he was actually a spy for the CIA. I think now about that bit of silliness and wonder if we were on to something, not about the CIA but about my father.

After breakfast I sit in my room and read until it's time for the courthouse to open up. There are names and dates I want to see written down.

In the first few hundred years of settlement, my English ancestors lived in a zoo of religious and ethnic groups who had little use for one another—Germans, Irish, English, Scots, and Dutch, Lutherans and Presbyterians, Quakers and Moravians, Mennonites, Anglicans, Schwenkfelders, Dunkards, Baptists, Catholics. The English in particular were suspicious and hostile toward them all, and everyone blamed everyone else for anything going wrong. Until they struck upon the idea of blaming everything on the 'savages,' who happened to be the only thing standing between them and possession of the continent.

The Europeans who came here had no ethnicity in common, no indigenous roots in the land, nothing to bind all of them together except greed and the hatred and fear of Native Americans, which was carefully cultivated for that reason. Eventually there was the nation-state and its symbols to provide a shared identity, the country becoming the government, the 'we' an 'it,' an institution with buildings and a flag and an anthem that hardly anyone can sing, and a budget and a monopoly over the use of force to compel obedience to the law and send us off to war.

It is nearly time, so I go out to the car to drive the short distance into town.

It is no surprise to me that the only time we act as though we are all in anything together is when the country goes to war, and we come to life as something resembling a People. There is, of course, some heroic pulling together when it's local—say, filling sandbags to save a town against a flood. But when it's national—an economic collapse, even global warming—it's everyone for themselves. A few months ago, as the economy slid into recession on its way to who knows what, there was a public television program on "How to Recession-Proof Yourself." Your*self*. Not how do we pull together to get our*selves*, our community, our nation, our People, through these hard times, but how do I and my nuclear family dig in, build a bunker, take the high ground so that even if everyone else goes down, we will be okay, as if that were possible.

If anything is sacred in this place, it is not the land or even God. And certainly not the flag, splashed across T-shirts and earrings, halter tops, baseball caps, beer cozies, beach towels, napkins, car ads, and a thousand other things I cannot think of at the moment. What is sacred is the belief in the idea of what the country was built upon, the right of every solitary, isolated individual to acquire as much property as they can. It was an idea that came rushing into the vacuum that was America unbound, the negative space of a vast expanse of possibility, but without a center from which to reckon who you are, who *we* are, what we owe, and to whom or what. There is no 'we.' 'We are all Americans' is another way of saying we are all eligible to engage in the same self-interested pursuit in the same political and economic landscape, a bunch of individuals out to achieve the American Dream for our*selves*, and everyone else is on their own. And anyone who doesn't like it is told to go someplace else, not getting the irony of it, that this is how it all began, hundreds and then thousands and then millions of people all going to the same somewhere else.

We are joined by a sentimentalized alienation in common, by the freedom to disregard anything that limits our ability to do whatever we want, including other people and nations and the land and everything that lives upon it. Don't tread on me. Live free or die. You're going too slow. Hurry up, move over, get out of my way.

Native Americans had no way to understand such an alien way of being. They did not realize what was coming after allowing Europeans to get a foothold on the continent. They did not know how deeply the newcomers envied their freedom and autonomy or that they would occupy the land in the way of the displaced and dispossessed and see themselves as God's chosen people, superior and civilized.

America, land of my birth, home to my mother's lineage for more than three hundred years, is the end result of centuries of compounded displacement and dispossession, both inside and out, which becomes the cultural ideal, it being all that is left, to be exquisitely and fabulously displaced and dispossessed. Americans will never be indigenous to this place, will never truly belong, because belonging is, more than anything, an attachment to the land, and while we have plenty of land—three hundred years of conquest and ethnic cleansing and genocide saw to that—there is no 'we' to attach.

It is easy to feel angry when I think of these things. I know the feeling well. I think anger is called for. But I also know that anger can come more easily than allowing myself to feel the grief of a broken heart. I pull the car to the side of the road and stop because I cannot see.

There are times when suddenly and without warning the earth takes on an outer edge and I fall right off into a void of abandonment and longing and despair. I used to think it was just an emotional thing, an old feeling rising up about my parents and what happened when I was small. Things did happen, and in real ways I was abandoned, but this feeling is about more than that and more than me. It is woven into the history of abandonment that brought all of us here—from the beginning a tide of refugees and slaves, the kidnapped and expelled, bringing only what they could carry, on their own, sink or swim, survive as best you can, pull yourself up by your bootstraps whether you have boots or not, don't let on that there is anything you cannot do without asking for help.

That is what I see in the photographs, a look of reserve bordering on hardness.

In such a land it is possible to indulge the illusion of being self-made, of self-invention. The wealthy and powerful in particular can imagine they do not need anyone at all and never did, that it's the other way around, we, the great mass, needing them.

It is also easy for everyone else to feel abandoned at one time or another, although difficult to admit, there being so much contempt for any sign of weakness or need.

Abandonment of workers losing their jobs, families their homes, of sick people whether they have insurance or not, of maimed and traumatized veterans coming home from war, of children bought and sold, women trapped with men who terrorize and beat them up.

For all the sentimental things we tell ourselves, for all the noble ideas that stand in for ethnicity, this has never been a nation where the people—everyone—truly came first, before the pursuit of power and wealth and profit and the interests of those who succeed at it.

This is why 'socialism' must be made a dirty word, to keep us from imagining something else, where people might actually matter, where the true disaster of New Orleans—what came *after* the hurricane—would be unthinkable. The communal society that Europeans saw in Native America and envied and praised and then destroyed, knowing what they were doing, that this is how you destroy a People and a way of life, a way of being, which is what they set out to do, consciously, with intent, and failing to appreciate the irony of trying to destroy a People by making them just like yourselves.

The courthouse is one of those large, stone, three-story government buildings designed to announce a going concern that is here to stay.

Inside I ask about land records and wind up in the auditor's office. When I tell the woman behind the counter what I'm looking for, she beckons to follow her into a small room off to one side, the walls lined with shelves of enormous books bound in leather. She scans a row and then pulls one down, laying it on the table in the center of the room. She takes the edge of the cover in both hands and opens it up and carefully turns over the pages until she finds the one she's looking for.

The top of the page reads 'Humbolt County, Iowa,' and below that are columns telling who sold what to whom and when, all done in a careful and elaborate script.

I ask her if these are original documents, just as they were created, and she nods, oh, yes, in a knowing and protective tone, like the curator in a museum.

She steps back and I bend down over the page to scan the column of names one

after another

until

there he is

Nils M. Johnson

I think I make a noise of some kind, although it could have been only in my mind, a sound to go with a surprise as much in spirit as in body or mind, as if something present in the name had drifted off the page and into the air to lightly come to rest around my heart.

My great-grandfather's name in a bound leather volume of public record. He was really here, stood behind the counter on April 12, 1871, a Wednesday, and watched the clerk write down in this very hand the names and the date and the exact location of the eighty-acre parcel that would root him and Margret to this place for the rest of their lives. They would be buried within sight of it.

And when the transaction was complete and the clerk closed the book with the same deliberate motion that had opened it just a few minutes before, my great-grandfather would have gone out the door to his horse and wagon to get on with the business of making the land his own.

Or what he believed to be his own, this being the European way, with ledgers and deeds.

The facing page continues with transactions over the next forty-six years as more land is acquired—in November 1885, another 80 acres, and then on two consecutive days in April 1888, 160 more, to make a total of 320 in all. And then, twenty-odd years later, the land is transferred to children as Nils becomes an old man following the death of Margret in 1908. My great-uncle Lars and his wife live with his father in the house that Loretta and I will see tonight.

While the clerk is photocopying the pages for me, I look about the room. There is a small mirror on the wall with a picture of President Eisenhower above a quote that reads, "America is great because she is good. And if America ever ceases to be good, America will cease to be great."

It is strange, this business of calling a nation 'she,' when you consider that when the United States has done anything, it has been men who directed and controlled it every step of the way. Then again, maybe that's the point.

As she hands me the copies, I ask if death records are kept here as well, and now she's off to another room and I can tell by the measure of her step that she is into it now and having a good time of it. She reminds me of librarians who love nothing more than tracking down an obscure reference to some long-forgotten bit of story that the person standing in front of them wants to know.

In the death record, my great-grandfather's nationality is listed as Norwegian even though he was a citizen of the United States. And his name is listed as 'Nels' instead of Nils, the name used in the land records right up to 1917, seven years before he died. He is also identified as Nels in the history of Humboldt County sent to me by the librarian. So, how did a lifetime of Nils turn into Nels at the end?

And then there is the puzzle of 'Nels' as my father's first middle name, which I'd think would have been Nils after his grandfather. Some in our family thought that's what it was when we were composing my father's obituary for the local paper. There was a dispute about the spelling of the name, which was resolved only when we dug out his passport and Social Security card, on both of which he was Nels. And yet still there was this confusion in the family, which turned out to have been around for a very long time.

Maybe it doesn't matter, the spelling of a name, except for not caring what they say about you as long as they get the name right. There are three versions of my own—Allan, Allen, and Alan—all of which differ from Nils and Nels in being pronounced the same. And yet it never ceases to annoy me to see it done wrong, because 'Allen' and 'Alan' are not simply misspellings of my name, they are also *not* my name. I am not Allen Johnson or Alan. You might as well call me George or Harry.

There are a few books of naturalization records on the shelf, which show multiple Nels Johnsons becoming citizens between 1873 and the 1890s, but not a single Nils. It doesn't come to much, since most of the volumes are missing. If only I could find a document that he'd had to sign himself, such as the title deed to his property, but the clerk says that would be in Des Moines.

Perhaps it is as simple as Nels being an Anglo version of Nils and the spelling's getting lost in the space between the grief of whoever reported the death and the clerk behind the counter who wrote it down.

I sit on a wooden chair in the corner and look at the rows of books on the shelves. I pull down the one for 1908 and find the death record for my great-grandmother, who is listed as Margrethe U. Johnson, born 1845 and died of carcinoma. Her father was Lars Ullensvang, no mention of her mother. Margarette, Margret, Margaret, Margrethe—one more thing lost in migration.

In the parking lot I ask a man where to get some lunch, and he suggests a barbecue place just down the road. I am disoriented, distracted and slow, almost hitting a car going out of the lot, the woman behind the wheel glaring at me, *what is the matter with you.*

The restaurant is friendly and heavy on linoleum and Formica and mashed potatoes and gravy. I order a small steak and baked beans. I know this food. It is my mother's.

I eat slowly, there being no place I have to be. I put my backpack on the chair beside me and take out a folder with photographs and documents that I threw together before leaving home. There is also a centennial book for the Lutheran church in Thor, which Loretta gave me on Sunday and I had put away and forgotten about until now.

On the first page is a photograph of the Ullensvang Lutheran Church in Hardanger, snow-capped mountains in the distance. On the next page are ministers going back to 1872, and then "Sons of Ullensvang Congregation who have entered the ministry" and there at the top, the first one, my grandfather in an old-fashioned oval frame. I am looking at his face, wondering what kind of man he was, what lies behind the smile, when I notice the name below

Johan Lewis Johnson

and wonder when was the moment that Johan decided to be John, and did he then shorten it to 'J. L.' to not be reminded of what he had done.

It seems to run in the family, this changing of names. I open the folder on the table beside me, and sifting through the photographs notice a small booklet with *Our Baby* written in blue on the cover and two holes in the spine where there once had been a piece of yarn or ribbon to hold it together. I remember this now, it being my father's, and open it, turning the first pages which are blank until the one that reads, "This place records the baby's name," and below, written in a careful script

Valdemar Nils Luther

I put the fork down on the plate and stare at the name of my father who was Nils after all, his grandfather's name, which, as it turned out, was not good enough for either one of them. What day was it, how old was Valdemar when someone asked the question or in filling out the form he paused over the matter of his name, and it did matter and he thought that he could choose, had to choose, and followed in his grandfather's and his father's footsteps and made that slight alteration that was so large.

I park on a shady side street near the Humboldt public library, where I find a computer and check my e-mail and do a search on Native Americans in Iowa.

The Sauk and Fox Nation endured a series of broken treaties strung out across the early 1800s. Black Hawk's War began in 1832, when hunters returned to find their villages occupied by white settlers who had driven the families away. They lost the war and Black Hawk was taken to the East Coast to impress him with the power and grandeur of the United States, which he was, returning home convinced of the futility of resisting the white invasion. His people were moved repeatedly until finally coming to something like rest in what would be the state of Kansas.

The Johnson farm and the Ullensvang cemetery are on the land of Sauk and Fox.

And Sioux, since the boundaries often shifted long before the coming of Europeans. But these were conflicts between peoples for the use of land in relation to which all were indigenous. What Europeans did—a nonindigenous people crossing an ocean to almost completely exterminate and remove indigenous nations from the land—was entirely different.

By 1850, everyone was gone from Iowa except for a few Sioux in the northwest corner, who would soon be driven north into Minnesota and South Dakota.

The state is named for the Iowa Nation, which just goes to show that conquerors get to take whatever they want, appropriate what appeals to them, even forgetting where it came from, as if it began with them. Then again, maybe it's a way of taking on what you most admire about those you have conquered, like eating your enemy's heart or liver in the belief that their power and virtue will become your own.

There were those who argued that the only way to save Native Americans was to fit them into the ways of whites—"to kill the Indian and save the man," as the founder of the Carlisle Indian School in Pennsylvania put it. The strategy included imposing the European practice of children's taking their father's 'last' name instead of having their own—no more Buffalo Bird Woman or Standing Bear or Medicine Horse.

Names were just the beginning of the campaign to destroy the social fabric by breaking apart bands and clans, forbidding the practice of Native religion, inculcating a desire for personal wealth, making a virtue of selfishness and putting yourself above the common good, competing with your neighbors, stamping out the sense of community based on a collective relationship with the land.

The real point was to take from Native Americans what land they still possessed. Perhaps the cleverest scheme of all—and the most devastating—was the Dawes Allotment Act of 1887, which forced the breakup of communal lands into holdings by individual families. Each got 160 acres, usually the least desirable portions held by the tribe. And then—this is the clever part—all the land that was 'left over,' the 'surplus,' was put on the market for white people to buy. The result was the takeover of more than twenty-eight *million* acres of Native American land, beginning with the Sisseton and Wahpeton Sioux reservation north of Hayti, South Dakota, where more than six hundred thousand acres were lost.

The steak and beans are forming a knot in my stomach. I have to get out of here, away from the computer and the books. I get up and go outside and walk around the neighborhood, trying to settle down.

They not only had their land and homes taken from them but also had to watch white people treat it in ways that were to them a desecration—slaughtering wildlife, tearing up the land in search of gold and silver, laying waste to entire forests, plowing up the grasslands that held the soil in place and fed horses and elk and buffalo. And every step of the way, white people treated them like children, saying it was for their own good, this destruction of everything that matters to a human being, declaring that the very thing they were doing was not their intention, was not what they were doing at all, and when they finally admitted to the fact, promising never to do it again before going on to do precisely that. Over and over.

How could Native Americans not want to drive the whites away, and how amazing it is that they held off for as long as they did, like Jews in the ghetto, full of denial and hope and disbelief that something so monstrous could be real. And when they did fight back, the outrage of whites at their effrontery, how *dare* you.

I remember hearing a story in the news about a woman one town over from our own who decided to keep honeybees and put the hive out in the open near the house. When a bear came, drawn by the honey, she shot and killed the bear.

And then there are the people who move out of the city to live in the woods and plant ornamental shrubs and complain bitterly when the deer come and eat them. There are too many deer, they say, they encroach upon us, we must kill off the surplus to keep the numbers down.

I sit on a bench across from a schoolyard where children are at play, noisy, laughing, calling out to one another. I close my eyes and focus on my breath, trying to ease the tightness in my stomach, the anger softening into sadness and then grief.

There was a time when all our ancestors lived on the land as Native Americans were doing before the Europeans arrived. A time before there was such a thing as Europe or English or Norwegian.

A weight of loss comes over me, and I open my eyes and am looking across the way at the children when it occurs to me that this feeling is more than mere emptiness. That it is a loss that cannot be permanent so long as there is someone alive to feel it. That grief contains the very thing it grieves, the love contained in the very mourning that it's gone.

I am sitting in my room at the hotel in the late afternoon, waiting for evening to come when I will meet Loretta at the house. How is grief possible with so much pressure to not give in to it, to cheer up, distract yourself, go buy something, see a movie, go to work, have some sex, get over it, turn on the TV. I feel the pull of the restless wandering of the truly lost, unable to stand still long enough to see my own dispossession and the truth of who I really am. Or am not.

The pursuit of happiness is at the heart of the American Dream, and yet when has happiness ever yielded to pursuit?

There is the story of the anthropologist who remarks to a southwest Native elder that all your songs seem to be about the rain, which must mean you worry a lot about not having enough of it. The elder thinks a moment and then nods and says, yes, it is true, and I notice that all your songs seem to be about love.

This room is clean and well-lighted and comfortable and cool in spite of the sun outside the window, and it has all the modern amenities—a refrigerator and microwave and cable TV and wireless Internet and a telephone I can use to call anyone anywhere in the world—and I cannot wait for evening to come so that I can get out of here, out of this emptiness in the midst of plenty. I could be anywhere—it makes no difference—which means that wherever I am is nowhere, no place, with no more reason than another for me to feel that this is where I belong.

My great-grandfather gave up his name to become part of this, the name that pointed him back to the village of Måkestad in the county of Ullensvang on the shore of Hardangerfjord. I believe he knew what he was doing, what it would cost, because he and Margrethe worked so hard to hang on for as long as they could. They spoke Norwegian at home and in church and ate lefse and lutefisk and yet, like the Native Americans whose land they now called their own, they must have known they could not win, that they could never go home again, and had to make the best of it by coming to believe it *was* the best.

But that was them and then, and this is now and me and my father's ashes in the corner and what to do.

I sit on the couch. I sit on the bed. I stand in front of the window and stare at the cloudy sky. I could eat something. There is free organic chocolate downstairs by the front desk, and she said to take as much as I like. I could turn on the TV. I could read a few pages in a book. But I cannot still my mind long enough to decide what to do, much less to do it. I try not to think about tomorrow because I have no idea. I remind myself that I planned it this way, a surplus of time, so that this very thing would occur and then I would have to see what comes out of it.

The people I meet are friendly and well-meaning, good people—no reason to believe they are not—the young woman at the front desk who gives me chocolate and lets me use the hotel computer to check my e-mail even though it's against the rules, the librarians, the clerks at the courthouse, the man who told me where to have lunch, the woman who waited on my table, the women who clean my room, and my relations who welcome me into their homes and, for a few days, a portion of their lives. History is not their fault or mine. We are caught in something that we did not set in motion but that now goes on in both the world and ourselves.

It occurs to me again how careful I am not to tell them why I'm here or what I'm thinking, what I write down in my journal when I pull the car to the side of the road. I do not tell them because I am afraid of the same things that made my great-grandfather give up his name, afraid of being misunderstood, eyed with suspicion, found out, shunned, excluded, not belonging, even to this thing, this nation, that at its heart is an embodied dispossession. I am afraid of being excluded from something that isn't even there, but, still, is all I have.

It amazes me how precarious and vulnerable is the status of being counted as a real American. Part of the deal is that you do not ask too much about it, you do not challenge your history teachers, you do not show up at school-board meetings and object to the use of Native American symbols and images as team mascots, you do not question the image of who we are that we have cultivated so carefully and for so long. You do not ask what being an American is all about beyond the land of the free and the home of the brave and a beacon of democracy and there is nowhere better on earth.

And you make clear your commitment to rooting out any signs of foreign identity or allegiance, losing the accent, the clothes, the hair, changing the name because you never know when it might be used against you. The German Americans who had been here for centuries and still had their homes attacked, their places of business vandalized during World War I because suddenly they were no longer counted as American. Or the likes of Emma Goldman, whose radical politics in the land of free speech were enough to revoke her citizenship and kick her out of the country. Or the Japanese Americans who were imprisoned in concentration camps, their homes and land taken from them, all without due process and while their sons fought and died in Europe. Or black people, who have never been treated as true Americans, from lynching and Jim Crow to World War II veterans denied the benefits of the GI Bill to Barack Obama, whose birth certificate was not enough to convince a vocal opposition that he was truly 'one of us.' And anyone with a face or a name or clothes that anyone else might construe as Arab or Muslim or Latino.

So much fear.

'American,' it seems, is both elusive and impermanent, something you are, or think you are, until someone says you're not, a license, a permit, an honorary membership that can always be revoked.

I have ancestors who came here more than three hundred years ago, and yet I can in the blink of an eye be told I am un-American because I oppose a war, and that I should leave and make my home in some other place. There are, it seems, no guarantees for any of us.

And yet I cannot deny that my whiteness does grant me a kind of immunity in comparison with all the rest. And the relative security that goes with it comes at their expense, because, without them, my whiteness has no meaning. The ease with which I move about this country as a white man, unchallenged, unscrutinized, cannot be separated from the lack of it among those who can be so easily excluded or cast out.

Still, I cannot escape the legacy of a country founded by masses of people who did not like it where they were and so went somewhere else, which happened to be here. And they have been moving ever since, looking for a better job, a friendlier town. So, 'love it or leave it' is not an invention of the sixties, when I first heard the phrase. It is a hallowed tradition, a core principle of the American Dream.

It is raining hard out my window and getting on toward 7:00 P.M., when Loretta will be waiting at the house. I look at the little brown box sitting on the bureau and feel time running out. What am I to do with you? Will it be tonight, in the rain? Where else is there except that small island in the middle of the prairie that drew your grandfather and grandmother from Norway across the sea, this scrap of the closest thing I can find to where you came from and might possibly belong.

I am not the cause of the displacement and dispossession that brought you and me to this place. And yet it does not matter, because here I am all the same, and even if this is the place for you, it may not be the one for me, if one exists at all. Too many generations gone by, too much lost, too much forgotten or never known to be remembered.

I had expected something more dramatic, the moment when it came to me, a sudden letting down in my body, bursting into tears, the revelation sharp-edged and unequivocal. But it is more quiet and subdued than that, a tap on the shoulder, a whisper, a presence padding into my mind, and then I am getting into the car and driving down the road in the direction of Fort Dodge to a hardware store I noticed coming in, where I will buy a tool small enough to hide but big enough to dig a hole.

The rain is letting up, the sun coming out from behind the clouds to make a rainbow over Thor. I drive south through the village and past the cemetery and then east to the house. Loretta's car is in the driveway beneath an old cottonwood tree.

The young couple who have bought the house from Heather greet us at the kitchen door. Heather and her husband made many improvements, but the feel of an old farmhouse is still intact, the high ceilings, the crown moldings. Standing in the dining room, I notice a doorway in the corner that I recognize from a photograph of my great-uncle Lars, the eldest son, and his wife, Elizabeth, sitting at the table. It would have been after Nils had died, the 1930s or 1940s. It startles me to make the connection between the photo and the people and the place and my standing here in this moment as time suddenly takes on its bent and circular nature and the house is full of people going on with their lives as they always have, children running on the stairs, voices high and rowdy against the measured words of parents. And somewhere in there is Johan—the name deep and softly rounded coming from his father's or mother's lips—who would turn himself into John.

We go upstairs. The hall is double-wide with windows at either end, an open space of its own, light and airy, a bureau along one wall. They show us the rooms, the plaster wall where Heather's grandmother drew a picture, the husband now trying to figure how to remove it for display.

I move slowly with the others, in my own world, unsure what the tears coming in are for—what I had and lost or what I never had at all or something else. But the pull is strong to whatever it is that inhabits this house.

We go downstairs and sit in the living room. Loretta tells the story of Selma, Johan's sister, who did not marry until she was in her seventies. There had been a young man she was attracted to, but they wound up going their separate ways until a half century later when he happened to show up at a funeral she was attending. They were married right over there, says Loretta, pointing to a corner of the room, where the piano used to be.

I ask to see the basement. I say something about how odd it is, wanting to see a basement, but no one seems to mind.

It is wet and dank, the walls made of rounded stone, and has the basement smell I love. There is a cistern in the corner, a small room with walls open at the top into which rainwater was funneled for use in washing and cleaning. I have never seen such a thing before. Nothing wasted. I used to think I got this tendency from my parents, but now I see how far back it goes.

We sit in the living room and talk as daylight comes down in the west. I glance at my watch, thinking I should go, wondering why the sense of urgency, it doesn't matter, it was meant to be in fading light, darkness coming on, the veil growing thin. And then it occurs to me that the voices in the room are keeping me here until the time is right, and so I give in, no hurry now, time making no difference at all.

I turn off the main road and drive slowly down the narrow lane into the cemetery. I get out of the car and turn in a slow circle, looking all around to make sure I am alone and unobserved. I watch a car move along the county road in the direction of Thor, anticipating the moment it turns in, headlights playing across the fields, found out, what are you doing here, who do you think you are sneaking onto land that was stolen from someone else.

Gray clouds move swiftly to the north, leaving behind a soft blue sky. Gentle birdsong rises from the earth beyond the grass and trees. The wind murmurs through the Black Hills spruce.

I take my backpack from the car and walk over to my great-grandparents' grave and sit down on the tombstone of my great-uncle Dan and great-aunt Elizabeth. I take the little brown box and the trowel I bought at the hardware store and set them on the ground.

I have done what I could with what I was given.

This is Valdemar, I say, little Valde, your grandson, my father, your boy.

And then I cry.

With the trowel I dig a plug of earth from the ground and hollow out the space to make room for the ashes. I take the plastic bag from the box and empty the contents into the hole. It seems so little, so quickly done. I replace the grass and work around the edges to seat it firmly so that no one will notice what I have done.

In my heart, I cannot make it right, to leave him here, and yet I have. As with so many before me, it seems the only thing to do.

I look out over the fields, losing track of time, slowly settling into the feeling of having crossed a line, that it is too late for anyone to undo what I have done, the ashes and the soil already becoming one and the other, impossible to tell apart. I sit back and light my evening smoke and watch a car move down the road. When I am done, I strip the remains of the cigarette and sprinkle the tobacco on the grave, bending down to say good-bye, my hand resting on the earth above my father.

As I drive back in the dark, the fields spread out on either side of the road, islands of trees silhouetted against the sky, dots of light showing from farmhouse windows, I imagine the solitary grove of trees out in the middle of the prairie and the voices now, soft and low, familiar, speaking in Norwegian.

I climb into bed and turn out the light and close my eyes and feel that I am alone in a way that I was not until just an hour ago, the room empty and large.

I sleep, dreamless, and in the morning go down for breakfast and then back up to my room where I sit on the couch and read two back issues of *USA Today* that I've had in my suitcase for almost a week. The news is like a soap opera that you can leave and always pick up again because so little has changed.

I go out to the car and get the empty box and bring it up to my room and put it in the trash. I will keep the trowel I used to dig the hole.

I drive to the library and send an e-mail to Nora, my first turn toward reentering the world, attending to the details of my life. My other life.

Already a strange and in-between kind of day.

I don't know why I do it, typing in the name of Nils M. Johnson and then clicking on 'search,' what I think I will find of this obscure Norwegian farmer, dead for all these years. Imagine my surprise when his name pops up in a website devoted to a book by Knut Gjerset with the title *Norwegian Sailors on the Great Lakes.* I recognize the author from a history of Norway that my father read in college and passed on to me several years ago.

My great-grandfather went to sea in 1855 when he was just sixteen years old, and took a year off to study navigation in 1861. He sailed from Bergen on the *Victor Immanuel*, loaded with emigrants to America, and then went on to Cuba and England and the Mediterranean. His last ocean voyage was another journey of emigrants, except this time he joined them and made his way to Chicago where he became a captain in the Great Lakes trade. His wife is named as Margaretha Larsdatter Ullensvang, adding a fifth spelling of her name and the middle name based on her father's, following tradition. When I think of her my mind stumbles, not knowing what to call her, this woman I am from.

I walk through the neighborhood, drawn again to children's voices in the playground, the sound of summer coming in, the last day of school, impending freedom in the air, emptying out my desk, the walk home.

I sit on a bench, no place to go, no one to see.

Shouldn't I be changed, a different person now? I seem to have established little beyond the fact that I do not belong in Iowa, no more than anywhere else.

My father was the last of his line, the last Norwegian passing as American, wandering the earth for almost a hundred years. If there was a map, he did not pass it on, not to me, but took it with him when he died. I doubt he knew what he was doing or could have helped it if he did. It was too much—married to a non-Norwegian whose parents looked down on him, this immigrant their daughter was hell-bent to marry, and then their own estrangement from each other, my father leaving my mother to raise us by herself. There was no way for me to grow up English or Norwegian or anything else but American.

So that is what I did in a way my father did not, as a 100-percent American. I never gave a thought to the question of what it really was that I was doing, which made it easier to be sure of it, to feel safe in it. Until now.

I wish my father could help me now, but that isn't going to happen and never was. Even if he were alive, I doubt he would have a clue about the strange place where I find myself or see it as a problem, being himself displaced for most of his life. But unlike me, which I did not know until just now, my father had a return ticket. Maybe his grandfather Nils slipped it into little Valde's pocket when he was lifting him into the wheelbarrow that Sunday afternoon not too many years before he died. And because of it, my father grew up knowing who he was and still knew it when he died, which is why, I suppose, he could say it made no difference, one grave as good as any other, all just portals out of this world, back to where you came from. Except for the difference between him and me, which I imagine it never occurred to him to consider.

Or maybe I am wrong about all of it, and I will never know.

The Humboldt Historical Museum is a farmhouse with period furnishings in the midst of a scattering of outbuildings—a barn, a one-room school, a Lutheran church. In the main house there is a picture on the wall of Pilgrims huddled together on the shores of 'New England,' somewhere in the crowd of faces a likeness distantly related to me.

I grew up and went to school believing this image told the entire story, good people yearning to be free, sustained by courage and faith, the sort of thing that lends itself to dramatic portraits and school pageants and presidential speeches. They never told us about the rest.

It is a nice house and well preserved, but there is nothing here for me, passing time.

In the photographs of my great-grandparents, everyone looks so stern, so tight-lipped, even Selma with her wild heart. I don't want to say they look hard, but they do. Nora said it's probably because the cameras were slow and you had to hold the pose for so long that it was easier to look grim than to hold a smile. Maybe that's all it was. Still, I wish I could see some softness. I cannot believe it isn't there, that there weren't times of tenderness or when they laughed themselves silly.

Then again, there is the joke about the Norwegian man who loved his wife so much that he almost told her.

I want to think of them as good people, kind, decent and honest, and innocent—that above all—unwitting pawns in a larger game, refugees with no idea of the land they were coming to and what had been done to make it possible. They came west across plains covered in grass six feet high, making their way through mud and swamps. They were afraid and had courage and heart and went to church and raised their children along with soybeans and corn and saved their money to buy more land. I want to believe that this is all their lives consisted of, hard work and heart and living out each day.

And maybe it is true. Maybe their lives were as simple and good as that. Perhaps they had no more idea of the truth of their adopted country than I did growing up in Massachusetts and going to school where betrayal and theft and genocide and ethnic cleansing never made it into the curriculum. I went to school for twenty years and came out with barely a clue. I was past sixty when it occurred to me to find out whose land we are living on and calling our own and how they came to have it taken away.

When Nils and Margaretha came to Thor, the real history had not been written and would not be for a hundred years. Manifest Destiny and the superiority of whiteness and all the entitlement that goes with it were taken for granted. All they had to do was make themselves fit in as white and work hard and have some luck, which they did and lived long lives and died with more than they had when they started, the American Dream.

And yet, while their lives were unfolding, it was only a matter of a few hundred miles over the horizon to the north and west where Native Americans, displaced and dispossessed, were scratching out their existence on the barren land that had been left them. To the south and east, black people were being terrorized and oppressed through lynching and Jim Crow and tenant farming. And while slavery had been formally abolished, the U.S. economic powerhouse could not have been built without it, just as it would not have happened without the removal of Native Americans. And that economy in the decades when my great-grandparents were establishing themselves in Iowa was providing huge urban markets for crops grown on the vast and fertile midwestern Plains.

I have no reason to believe that my great-grandparents were not good people who worked hard for everything they had. Nothing in the history of this country can take that away from them or from me.

If only that were the whole of it. If only it did not matter that they were prospering and building their lives on stolen land in the midst of the ongoing brutal legacy of racism and slavery. If only it were enough to say they did not do the stealing, the enslaving, the cruelty, the murder, did not know the ones who did, had no idea.

Loretta says there is a restaurant in Thor—the only commercial establishment in town, as far as I can tell—that I should not miss. It goes by the name of Unkies and serves a steak that people come from miles around to eat.

I arrive a few minutes before 5:00 P.M. The outside of the building is as plain and unassuming as everything else out here. I am walking to the door when I hear a voice call out from across the street, "You still trying to find your relations?"

It is Roger, the man with the memory, doing some late-day demolition work on a brick building that seems to have collapsed in on itself.

I look at him and smile, "I am."

"Any luck?"

"Enough." I cross the street and we talk awhile about names, starting out as one thing, ending up another. I point out that Nils did not have his first name spelled out on the tombstone, just the initial, a mystery right down to the last.

We shake hands, we say good-bye.

Before going back to the hotel, I stop at the cemetery beneath a gray sky and have my evening smoke while sitting beside the little hole I dug for my father.

A hypothetical: What if I were going to die without a new kidney and they could not find a donor and then at the last minute one was found and my life was saved. And what if, years later, I found out that the origin of the kidney that made it possible for me to live and prosper had been forged. What if I learned that it had been taken from a young woman who had initially been offered money in exchange for one of her kidneys but when she refused was murdered to take her organs for the black market that profits from desperate people such as me? What if it were done by white men to a woman who was black or Latina or Native American because they believed a white person's life was worth more than any person's of color?

How would I not be haunted by this for the rest of my life? How would I reconcile every happy moment with the terror and suffering that had been inflicted on her so as to make those moments possible for me? I am innocent. I have done nothing wrong. And yet it can never be as simple as that.

I put my hand on the little patch of ground that is now my father's grave. I tell him that I love him, calling him 'Papa,' saying that I will come to see him tomorrow before I leave, pretending that he can hear, that it matters.

Behind me the Black Hills spruce moves softly in the wind.

Driving north on the road through Thor, a car passes by, in a hurry, the driver holding a cell phone to his ear. I watch him accelerate through town, feeling myself between worlds.

Loretta invites me to lunch with Ron and Jim on my way to Minneapolis. I stop at the cemetery to say good-bye, which seems odd in the moment after I have said it, what it means, and yet it is what comes out as I am standing there looking down. Good-bye.

I wonder if I am the first person in my lineage to inquire in this way into these lives, and will I be the last.

And why me, why now?

I look out over the fields to the farmhouse in the distance. Someday it will be gone. Heather had a hard time finding a buyer. It will only be harder when the price of farmland is higher still. Who will want to live in such a house, sit on the front porch in the evening and look out through the trees to the fields across the road, when the land could be growing corn for ethanol instead? In my mind I hear the voices of children and parents calling after. But none of it is real. I have no special knowledge of this place, no claim, no right to be here. I came to leave my father, which I am about to do. I will drive away and not come back. This was for him, and for me only to resolve a dilemma. It did not matter, is what he said, and yet it mattered to me that it did not matter to him. I needed to know why, and perhaps I do, although it is difficult to see through the loneliness that comes over me now, holding in my hand the end of a broken chain.

I am leaving you, and yet why do I feel that I am the one who is left?

At Loretta's house we sit in the dining room and eat and talk about what is happening to farms and to the land, what it means to be American. It occurs to me that my great-grandparents, like so many millions of immigrants, did not come to this place because they wanted to be American, to no longer be Norwegian. They came because they heard they could make a better living here, a captain's pay on the Great Lakes being far more than shipping out of Bergen. They took on the appearance of this emerging identity called 'American' only because it allowed them to stay and shielded them from discrimination and hostility and exclusion from the American Dream. And they did so reluctantly, holding out against assimilation for generations, opening their own schools and churches and mutual-aid societies, publishing books and newspapers in their native languages to remind them of who they were and would remain for as long as it was possible.

We say good-bye. We take pictures of each other in front of the house. We shake hands, and I feel how much I like these people. I wave from the car as I pull away.

When Europeans invaded this continent, they did not give themselves up to the land and its people but thought they could by brute force and the favor of God make themselves the People of this place. But you cannot be from a land you know nothing about, and for all our science and geography, I doubt we have ever had any idea of where we really are.

We cannot all just be Americans in America, because there is no such thing.

This is the price to be paid by a descendant of those who invaded to displace and dispossess and exterminate—to live out an illusion full of longing for what my ancestors have made it impossible to have. It is also a legacy passed down from immigrants, to be far from home and unable to return—there being no vessel swift enough to sail back in time—and to forget who we are and then forget we have forgotten.

The road north is a divided highway, which I have tried my best to avoid, but I am feeling done and wanting to get where I am going, the house of my cousin Jim, where I will stay the night before flying home in the morning. There is traffic and noise, and I can feel myself reentering the world. The sun comes out from behind the clouds. I turn on the air conditioner but not the radio.

In St. Paul, Jim and Bill and I go out to dinner. I tell them some of what I've seen and found but keep most of it to myself, the talk light and friendly, which is easy given how little we know of each other.

There is hunger and envy and sadness that come up in me when I hear their stories of trips to funerals of relatives I have not heard of until now, visits to great-aunts and uncles, the things they left behind.

I was born in this country, and yet my grief is still an immigrant's grief.

In the middle of dinner, it suddenly dawns on me that I forgot to go into the basement of the church in Thor to see the documents and photographs they had gathered for the anniversary. I cannot believe I could have been so . . . what? . . . feeling stupid and embarrassed, staring down at my plate, absently turning over a piece of food with my fork, waiting for this to pass. I try to rejoin the conversation, the back of my mind still working it out . . . that I will never go there again, that it is too late and whatever is there I simply will not see, like the house in Hayti . . . and then a calm coming in to replace the panic at having come all this way only to get it wrong, realizing now that nothing is there that would make a difference.

After dinner we drive by the house where my grandparents lived out their retirement. My grandfather died in 1948, two years after I was born, and I wonder how he is named on his tombstone—Johan, John, J. L., this need for an alias, to be also known as someone else, the cardboard cut-out that looks just like yourself, the altered name, the covered past, the strange company of spies and criminals and serious writers who don't want anyone to know they wrote those trashy novels. And immigrants and their children for generations out.

My grandmother lasted until 1957. I may have met her once—my sole contact with any of my grandparents—when we came home from Norway in 1954. I was only eight years old at the time, and all I have is the memory of a very old woman sitting in a chair like a queen holding court and me coming forward to say hello. I don't remember what she said or if she touched me. I do recall that the lighting in the room was dark, perhaps a cloudy or rainy day, and I could not see her face clearly in the dim light.

I ask Jim and Bill about the subject of ethnicity and where we are from and my father saying he was Norwegian. They doubt their father would have said the same, which surprises me, although I don't know why I should be surprised. Jim goes on to say he doesn't feel he has any ethnicity at all, which takes us into the question of what you call a nation without ethnicity, a place where no one is from—a collection of city-states, an open market, a headquarters for corporations, an off-shore casino, but in any case, a going concern, a place of business, to paraphrase Calvin Coolidge. Or Bill Clinton. *It's the economy, stupid.*

We sit around the kitchen table and talk into the night. When I finally go to bed, my mind won't settle down.

Jim said something about the violence and hatred that coalesce around ethnic differences, that perhaps ethnicity is something we could do without and there being no American ethnicity might be a plus. But then what do we hang on to for a sense of identity and belonging to something larger than ourselves, which human beings seem unable to do without? What is left is the nation-state and patriotism and our tendency to come together only when we go to war, so I cannot see how that's any better, if not worse.

My plane doesn't leave until early afternoon, so I suppose it won't matter if I sleep. I can lie here and think all night if I want.

Somebody is always conquering somebody, one of them said when I brought up the subject of Native American land. There is nothing unusual about our history, we are not the only ones. That's true enough, except it's not the story we tell ourselves and the rest of the world.

Alexis de Tocqueville wrote that American democracy was dangerous because its citizens have such an inflated opinion of themselves precisely because their form of government is so much better than the rest. We are prone to believe we can do no wrong, make well-intentioned mistakes, perhaps, but do no *wrong*, nothing to make us feel ashamed. We tell ourselves we are better than everyone else, that the whole world wants nothing more than to be like us, to *be* us, and if they don't, it is because they are ignorant or envious or stupid, all the more proof of our superiority. And the 'we' and the 'us' and the 'our' are, still, invariably defined as white.

I sit up in bed and look out the window at the dark street. The house is quiet and still. All the things I know, and yet how can they mend a broken heart?

I want to be Dorothy and click my heels three times, take me home, there's no place like home, which is what I came here to find, a place deeper than the town and the three acres of land where I live, a place of origin and not just people but *a* People who every time I look at them or hear them speak, remind me of who we are, what we are about, where we are from. I have wanted some bit of magic, for the land to speak and claim my soul. Perhaps it did and I wasn't listening. It would not be the first time. And perhaps it was a conversation that was supposed to begin with me. But how am I to know?

I have wanted to bring home some attachment, a belonging to something larger than myself or my family, but all that I have found is kind relations and a little bit of soil in which to plant the remains of my father, in the midst of an ocean of stolen land and stolen lives and dreams, leaving me feeling more lost than when I began.

I should have been Norwegian, but I am not. I am a white American who does not know how to attach himself to that without living a lie.

When Michelle Obama said that for the first time in her life she felt proud of her country, it sounded to me like an occasion for celebration, a black person able to have a moment of feeling proud of a country that has treated black people so badly and for so long. Instead, the criticism came down on her like a storm, how unpatriotic of her, how disloyal. And I realize now that the critics were right, that she was disloyal, but not to what they thought. She was disloyal to the silence, to living the illusion, the fantasy that is the real American Dream. At your peril do you point out that this country was *founded* in part on persecution and oppression and the enslavement and torture of millions of human beings, creating masses of refugees driven from their homelands by violence and intimidation organized against them.

I am so agitated that I have to get out of bed. I stand in front of the window. I don't know what to do with myself. There are hours to go before daylight. I would go outside and have a smoke if there weren't the chance of waking Jim in his room just down the hall. I would probably set off the burglar alarm.

breathe

When I hear of a horrible crime—such as a man murdering his wife and child—I often remind myself that it is someone's boy who has done this terrible thing. Having children of my own, I sometimes wonder what I would do, what I would feel, if I were the one who had raised this child and known him as good and kind. How would I love him then? How could I forget and deny the horror that he had done and still fully and truly love the man who did it? And what would become of me, who had raised him into the man who was the source of such pleasure and pride but also this? How could I feel a connection to all the good that came of that without also embracing the rest? Would I get to pick and choose? Would I say to myself it would be disloyal or unloving to speak or even think about the horror that he did, and so do not, go on as if it never happened, never mattered, was done by someone else?

I think I would have to make myself a little crazy to do that.

It might help to think of the Europeans who came here early on, including some Dudleys, Griswolds, and Baileys, as being a little crazy from the start, boatloads of refugees, convicts, kidnapped children, slaves, adventurers, conquistadores, entrepreneurs, all pouring in together, frightened, hungry, dirty, smelly, greedy, unable to grow their own food, suspicious of one another, fresh from a Europe awash in oppression and misery and the chaos of religious war and torture driven by the brutal arrogance of kings and the righteous.

It does not excuse what they did, but it does provide a little perspective.

I am so tired. I want only to sleep, to be unconscious, to go home, to forget, to have never known.

When Nora and I went to Washington to see the new Museum of the American Indian, we found many beautiful things, and there were moments when I felt moved by what I saw. But I could not help but notice how hard I had to look to find the few sentences on the wall that mentioned the history of conquest and genocide, removal and broken treaties, how easy it would be to come away with no idea of that at all.

Self-knowledge is always bad news. I heard that on a tape of Steven Levine's, who wrote *Who Dies?* and works with people who are dying. Something is dying inside me that needs to die, a phantom of longing masking grief.

I know this feeling—that it would kill me to look at the truth, really look at it, say it out loud, as if the words would turn me to stone. I know it in the way my mouth can refuse to move in the moment of admitting something wrong, of apology. And I remember seeing it in my mother's face many years ago when she and I would argue about history and what the English had done and she did not want to hear of it, shaking her head and holding up her hands to ward it off as if I were talking about her and not our ancestors who've been dead for two or three hundred years. As if I were talking about *her*. And *me*. No wonder it's so hard to have a serious conversation about the ugly side of history with so much at stake.

I have never known denial to make me stronger. What it does is suck the life from me by making it impossible to live in what is real.

It is a desolate and lonely place that can feel like self-hatred, that I am not good enough to live in reality.

To disown history is to disown the people I came from and I cannot do that without losing some part of myself. Nothing is past. Everything is here, coming round and round, wanting only to be seen, to be claimed, brought in.

When something is founded on a lie, on murder, on betrayal, on cruelty and injustice, duplicity and greed, it does not matter what else went into it or how good it turns out to be. The one does not balance out the other. It is not possible to separate the end from the beginning, which is why so much hard work is put into forgetting, moving on, denying it ever happened, turning it into something else.

I am one of those who have deep feelings about the 'experiment' that is called the United States of America, about the Constitution and the Bill of Rights, and Concord and Lexington and the bravery in laying everything on the line. And the resilience of the human spirit that I see in the eyes of my ancestors staring out from the photographs. But I cannot claim the pride of my connection to the good that has come of them and the history of this place without also claiming the bad. I had nothing to do with either and am equally deserving and undeserving of both. It is all or nothing.

I climb into bed, drawn to a sleep that even my busy mind cannot resist. I think of my father, the sound of his voice, the look on his face when he spoke Norwegian, sang the songs, told the stories. And then I remember when he visited Nora and me just after we built our house in the woods, how he walked the land and the feeling that came over me when he looked around and said that it reminded him of Norway, how it made me smile, and the small cloud of sadness that came after.

A life is a set of intersecting stories branching out beyond what we know in one moment or the next, going back in time farther than we see or imagine, no beginning, middle, or end, winding, looping back, going far, drawing near. Nothing is simply in the past or the present, history not a thing to remember or forget or repeat.

My father is dead and he is also alive in the room, the little boy, the old man, the one who was my father. He is present as the bed is present or the window or my hand, because his whole life was there in what he said when I asked my question, in the words and the shrug and whatever was going on behind his eyes that did not look at me. His whole life was in that moment passing into me, the one who asked the question because it was mine to ask, and I was there to receive not only what he had to say but also the life from which it came. And I have been carrying it ever since, the essence of my father, which I cannot put down or leave behind or bury in a little piece of ground.

My father is here, and Nils and Margaretha are crossing the prairie, and the horror is being done while the silence goes on in the killing of a dream. And yet there is also something else, what the poet Jane Kenyon called "perfect possibility," because the past is not past, never over, never done.

Jim and I have a quiet breakfast before he goes off to work and leaves me in the house for a few hours before I leave for the airport. I finish packing and then sit for a long time—I don't know just how long, it being that kind of sitting and staring out the window. I have traveled across centuries and generations and almost two thousand miles since I landed in Minneapolis ten days ago, and it seems I haven't been anywhere at all, perhaps because no matter where I go, I always take myself along.

At the airport I buy a copy of the *New York Times* to read while I'm waiting for the plane. The page-one headline reads, "Food Is Gold, Investors Pour Billions into Farming." Speculators and corporations and hedge funds are buying up farmland and grain elevators, consolidating 'small holdings' for the sake of economic 'efficiency.' The tone of the article is positive and upbeat, the author convinced that this is a wonderful thing for the benefit of all. There is no mention of what happens when powerful groups control all our food or about the disappearance of small farms and towns or about cutting down trees that keep the topsoil from blowing away or the future of a corporate industrial model of agriculture that works only so long as oil is cheap.

On an inside page is an article about Monsanto's program of genetically engineering seed that it patents as a form of life, reserving to itself the right to forbid farmers to set aside some of their crop each year to seed the next.

First the land, then the water and the food.

I fold the newspaper in my lap and watch people going by.

Past is present, present past.

The Lakota called the white people *Wasi'chus*, the greedy ones who take the fat.

Crazy Horse could not imagine why someone would even think they could sell "the earth upon which the people walk."

His real name was Tashunko Witko.

Sitting Bull was Tatanka Yotanka. "We want no white men here," he said. "The Black Hills belong to me. If the whites try to take them, I will fight."

I close my eyes as the plane lifts into the air, feeling strange and out of place, not knowing how to be, as if I have forgotten the rules and conventions and the tricks of forgetting and denial that make it possible to fit into a way of life, to get along, pass by undisturbed.

The engines strain against the pull of the earth growing smaller beneath us and yet also larger.

The sky is blue outside the window, massive white clouds passing down below. We are flying to the east. If we keep on going out over the ocean and make a slight turn left, we will wind up over England and then Norway. Just there beyond the curvature of the earth.

The flight attendant is handing out drinks and trays of food in first class, smiling, making conversation. A woman next to me is reading a book, a man beside her sleeping by the window. Another man works on his laptop in the row in front of me, across the aisle, and in the row beyond a girl is watching *The Wizard of Oz.*

Anyone I might ask would probably agree that we are all in this moment living in reality. Except if I point out how little separates us from several miles of air, how tiny a dot we are up in the sky, how little it would take—a flight of birds sucked into the engines, it has happened before—to lose our hedge against gravity and plummet to the earth, if I said something about how thin the floor is beneath our feet, and then the cargo bay and the skin of aluminum under that. If I were to point out how little there is between us and the wild blue yonder outside the window, I can imagine the nervous smiles, rolling eyes, the quick return to the book, the nap, the movie, the meal, the trappings of denial.

I look at the people around me. We may all die together this afternoon on the way to Hartford, Connecticut, perhaps somewhere over Ohio or Pennsylvania. I am not being silly or morbid. Planes do crash, and there is no reason for the next one not to be the one we're on today. These might be the last faces I ever see, the last voices that I hear. I feel a tenderness for all of us when I consider how vulnerable we are, not simply way up here in the sky but as human beings, anywhere and all the time. You think you have a life, that it will go on, and why not? And then you get up one morning, a good morning, like all the rest, and go down to the edge of the sea and look out and notice a dot of white on the horizon, which you have never seen before, cannot imagine as you wonder what it is, what sort of bird, what it will bring.

I do not want us to die, not here, not now, but the us that I want to go on living is nothing more than a collection of human beings who happen to be in the same place at the same time. There is no reason to assume we all speak the same language or know the same history, have the same feelings about the same piece of land, are from the same place, the same People. And yet it is a safe bet that most would say they are American. I imagine getting out of my seat and going up and down the aisle and asking where you are from, not where you live or where you were born, but where, deep in the knowing of your heart, you are *from*, and then the quizzical look, the narrowing eyes, the disarming simplicity sinking in. I am not smug about this. I would look no different. But it would be nice to have some company.

The flight attendant is coming down the aisle with soft drinks for the rest of us, while up in first class the passengers shake out napkins and accept another glass of wine.

If the plane goes down, there will be an instant when we know that we are going to die right here and now. And in that space of time, we will none of us be any different from anyone else on the earth at that same moment in a life, whether now or a million years ago, or any different from an animal coming to meet its death, the caribou brought down by the wolf, the cow entering the chute, the bird falling to the ground. All boundaries dissolve and there is no human, no animal, no Mohawk or Norwegian, only the universal crying out, the sudden gasp, the astonishment of being, felt only in the imminence of not.

I take some comfort in knowing this, to be a human being on the earth, filling in a portion of what I feel missing in myself. I wish it were enough. Perhaps there will come a day when it is.

Sometimes you ask and the answer is no. And sometimes the only answer is the silence around the beating of your heart.

Sometimes the only place is no place at all but where you are.

Sometimes justice is all there is to hang on to, and truth the only ground to stand upon. And compassion, without which we cannot bear the truth or find the justice.

I close my eyes.

I could love a People brave enough to value justice and truth more than coming out on top, brave enough to be afraid, to stand before the mirror and not blink or flinch or turn away, wise enough to ask forgiveness for things they have not done, to put out the fire they did not start, to restore the balance of all things by atoning for what must be atoned and by us because there is no one else.

Sometimes I think I could stand on what I believe as a kind of ground, but it is not the same as what I came all this way to find. I want something more than to be white in North America, where for hundreds of years the dream has been the freedom to go wherever you want and do and take whatever you can, where compassion is a weakness and greed a virtue and justice means getting what you want. *Wasi'chu.* But I am destined not to have it, and now I understand a little more of the peculiar loneliness that has dogged me all my life.

Outside the terminal, I see the car and the darkened form of Elsie Bean pacing back and forth. Nora sees me coming, smiles and waves, lowers the window so that I can put my face against Elsie's cold wet nose as she sniffs me in, returning me to the pack. Sliding into the passenger seat, I am suddenly more tired than I have been in weeks. I am happy to be back and yet also sad to have left wanting so much that I did not know and to return with what seems so little.

Several years ago, Nora and I sat at our dining room table as she looked through a genealogy sent by one of her relations. She was browsing, flipping pages, when she looked up at me to say she had found a Griswold, and did it mean that we're related? I don't know, I said, but I imagine that it does, Griswold not being the sort of name that people would adopt, like Smith or Johnson.

I get my copy of a genealogy that was given to me by my sister several years before, and Nora calls out names and dates. It is one of those small but astounding moments when I see the name, a small piece of a vast mechanism clicking into place, and then we are both of us going back and forth working our way through generations that finally converge on the family of Michael and Ann Griswold who settled in Wethersfield, Connecticut, in 1640. They had nine children, including two sons who grew up to be great-great-great-great . . . grandfathers to Nora and to me.

There was something miraculous in this, to have been so close for almost thirty years and only now discover that we were closer still than we ever knew or imagined. We are cousins, we whispered to each other across the table, like sharing a delicious and slightly wicked secret. Is this why we felt like familiars from the start? Is it possible?

I sit on the deck and look out into the woods over the land of the Massacoe and have my evening smoke.

Elsie comes and lies in her favorite spot in the corner, sniffing the air. She turns her head to a sound, as do I, a large animal walking among the trees, a deer or a bear. I stand, and Elsie and I are very still in this moment of discernment, and then the deer emerges from the shadows, making her way up the hill. We watch until we cannot see her anymore.

In the stillness it comes to me that we own this piece of land only in relation to other human beings. Otherwise it no more belongs to us than to the deer and fox and bear who also make their home in these woods.

A man in the next town over came upon a black bear in his garage one afternoon, which he had carelessly left open with birdseed stored inside. The bear did what a black bear does, accepting the invitation to dine and then, realizing her mistake, ran away, having come to eat and not to fight. But the man was having none of that and went into his house and came out with a gun that he used to shoot and kill the bear as she fled into the woods beside the house.

The bear was a sow with two cubs who would not survive without their mother.

The man said he had a right to defend his property, his little bag of seed, and there were many in the town who agreed.

He was arrested, which I was pleasantly surprised to hear, but his punishment was only to pay a fine of a few hundred dollars, which I was not.

I grieve the bear and I grieve her cubs, who went off to die alone in the woods. I grieve the culture that would make of their deaths something so small, that would give a frightened, angry, vengeful man the idea that his bag of seed is worth more than the lives of bears.

Many Native Peoples regard the bear as a sacred animal, noting how similar it is to humans in its manner and the makeup of its body. I once dreamed of a bear, a cub who came near to me in the night. I leaned down and placed my fingers in her mouth, which she seemed to want me to do, and I felt the fine sharpness of the baby teeth but was not afraid, knowing the bear would do no harm to me.

A few nights later, I woke to the sound of the dogs putting up a ruckus downstairs. It was early spring and there was still snow on the ground. I called out to them to be quiet but their barking only grew louder and more urgent, which had never happened before, so I went downstairs and stood beside them at the window and looked out into the open space beside the house. And there in the moonlight was a small black bear silhouetted against the snow.

I called up to Nora, excited, "it's a bear," and she replied, in a hush that, "no, there are two."

A mother and her cub.

I felt myself six years old again, transfixed by the sight of them as they danced and cavorted in the moonlight, their fur shiny black, their movements fluid and smooth and muffled by the snow and the windows closed against the cold. They went across the front of the house through the garden and back again and then were gone into the night.

There was another time later on, perhaps that same year, I don't remember, when we woke again in the middle of the night, but this time to the sound of boards being snapped in two. Nora was out of bed in a flash, worried about her goats in the small barn a short distance from the house.

It turned out to be a bear ripping at the board and batten to get inside the barn.

We went out onto the front porch, Nora yelling and banging a spoon on an old kitchen pot while I shouted and shined a light. The bear stopped what she was doing and turned in our direction and stood up on her hind legs to her full height, which nearly reached the bottom of the roof line. I stepped down off the porch. I don't know why I was not afraid, this being the closest I had ever been to a wild animal that was so much bigger than a man. She was magnificent standing there, quiet and still, trying to get the measure of me. Well, hello, I said, because that is what came to me to say, and then, perhaps to get a better look, I shone the light into her face, which she didn't like at all and promptly turned and ran off into the woods.

We repaired the damaged boards and went back to bed. A few hours later, the bear was back again, and out we went, banging and shining until she went away.

At first we feared the bear was after the goats, but more likely she was drawn to the sweet grain in the feed room, which we then moved to the garage. Some time later, we installed an electric fence. Nora also made a point of asking the bear to stay away, which, as far as we can tell, she has. We have mixed feelings about that.

Why am I thinking about the bear? It has to do with this place, the land, the feeling that I have when I come back to it. And then I think of another piece of land and my father's ashes that seem so far away in that little grove of trees in the middle of Iowa.

It is good that I did what I felt called to do. And I am glad to be here again and alive. I feel free of a weight of illusion I have carried all my life and yet also troubled by what there is to take its place.

Someday my children may ask where they should spread my ashes when I am gone. I expect I will hear the question differently than I did when I asked my father, and if I also do not know what to say, it will have new meaning. Perhaps we will talk and discover what I cannot see on my own. Or perhaps I will tell them that they will have to find the place where I belong as the only way to know about themselves what they do not know now, and that my telling them, even if I could, would not be heard in the way the voices came to me from over the cornfields that evening not so long ago. I know my answer will not satisfy. They may tell me it is unreasonable or unfair, too much to ask. And maybe they'll be right and maybe that won't change a thing. Maybe it does not matter one way or another so long as we do what we are called upon to do.

Perhaps I will remember to tell them what my father did not tell me, may not have known to tell, that it does matter but in ways we must find out for ourselves.

This being close to the end of the story, I know that here is where I am supposed to reveal the solution to the problem I posed at the beginning, or at least bring some sense of closure, if not the happy ending that my father always wanted to find at the close of one of my novels but did not.

Here is where I might reveal that things were not as hard as they seemed when I set out. Or that the thing I went to find was really with me all the while, or maybe something out of T. S. Eliot, that at the end of our explorations we wind up back where we began and know it for the first time, that I needed only to go away and come home again to realize what I have had all along.

Or I might suddenly realize that as a human being, the earth itself is my home, that I belong wherever I happen to be, that my humanity is all I need to define my place. I know people in my position who find some comfort in this idea, who believe ethnicity and place are less than they are cracked up to be. Better to be free to go anywhere you want and still call it home.

There are times when such thinking can find a congenial place in my mind, the human mind that is so adept at making things up and treating them as true. But my heart, my body, knows better, and sooner or later it will assert the knowledge that belonging is not an idea but a reality of body, where feeling resides, and place.

And now it comes to me that of course my father was right. For him it made no difference, being so thoroughly and unalterably Norwegian in a way that was lodged so deep inside that it may never have occurred to him unless someone were to ask, as I did that day. I expect his soul found its way home long ago to dance in the waterfalls cascading down from the mountains every spring, falling home into the waters of Hardanger.

But I am not my father.

I look out into the darkening woods. I am a man who knows happiness. I love my family and I love my friends and the animals who live with us and nearby. I love these woods, this house, more than any place I know. And I am a white man in North America, far from home and perhaps as close as I will ever be.

ACKNOWLEDGMENTS

Note: My reference to T. S. Eliot is from his poem "Little Gidding," in *Four Quartets*; my reference to Jane Kenyon's "perfect possibility" is from her poem "Afternoon in the House" in *Otherwise.* The quote from Mary Rose O'Reilly is from *The Love of Impermanent Things.* The quote from the governor of Georgia on the subject of treaties with Native Americans can be found in James Wilson, *The Earth Shall Weep: A History of Native America.*

From its beginning, this journey was for me a leap of faith, and everywhere I went, I was met with kindness and a generosity of spirit I will not forget. I am deeply grateful to my cousins, Jim and Bill Johnson, Loretta (Lothe) Baker, Jim Lothe, and Heather Fogelman, and Loretta's husband, Ron, for welcoming me into their homes and lives and helping this long-lost relation discover something of where and whom he is from. And I am thankful to Roger with the long memory and to the man in the restaurant who responded to the disclosure of my search with such unadorned humanity and grace.

I thank all those who gave of their time and skill so that I might find my way into my family's past, especially the librarians and county clerks in Humbolt, Iowa; Tom Ellig, director of the Lower Sioux Agency Museum; and the assistants in the Wells and Hayti Lutheran churches. I thank Pastor Randy Eisenbeisz for our thoughtful conversation and for sending me farther west beyond the trees and Pastor Chris Lang for welcoming me with such an open heart. I am especially grateful to Zoa Heckman, without whose kindness and inspired persistence I would not have found the house where my father was born.

Closer to home, I am indebted to Ellen Allen, Annie Barrett, Anne Batterson, Kristin Flyntz, James Harrod, and Rob Okun for their abiding friendship and support, and to my sister, Annalee Johnson, for, well, being such a sister to me for as long as I can remember, in ways that helped make this journey possible. And Nora Jamieson, my partner in life who has been with me every step of the way for more than thirty-five years, who saw me off and welcomed me home, it is hard—no, impossible—to imagine a life without you and your love and courage and wisdom in the search for what it means to be a human being.

I am grateful to the staff at Temple University Press for all that they have done to make this book a reality. Special thanks go to my editor, Aaron Javsicas, for his thoughtful and steadfast belief in the work; to Alex Holzman and Janet Francendese for their timely support and encouragement; to Gary Kramer, publicity manager, Irene Imperio Kull, advertising and promotion manager, and Ann-Marie Anderson, marketing director, for their skill and dedication to bringing the book to an audience of readers; and to Joan Vidal, production editor, Kate Nichols, art manager, and Heather Wilcox, copy editor, who guided the book into print with such care and good spirits. They are together the best example I have known of what publishing is all about.

I also want to thank George Yancy and Becky Thompson for their thoughtful reviews of the manuscript, and Ellen Chulak for an artful and fruitful brainstorm.

In addition, I am indebted to the following whose work, along with that of many others, shaped my experience on this journey:

Theodore W. Allen, *The Invention of the White Race: Racial Oppression and Social Control*
Russell Banks, *Cloudsplitter*
Dee Brown, *Bury My Heart at Wounded Knee*
Nigel Davidson, *The African Slave Trade*
W.E.B. Du Bois, *The Souls of Black Folks*
Anne Farrow, Joel Lang, and Jennifer Frank, *Complicity: How the North Promoted, Prolonged, and Profited from Slavery*
Marilyn French, *Beyond Power: On Men, Women, and Morals*
Knut Gjerset, *Norwegian Sailors on the Great Lakes*
Hamlin Historical Committee, *History of Hamlin County, South Dakota*

Historical Publishing Company, *History of Humboldt County, Iowa*
Valdemar Nels Luther Johnson, *From the Prairie to the Ocean*
Don Jordan and Michael Walsh, *White Cargo: The Forgotten History of Britain's White Slaves in America*
Stephen Kinzer, *Overthrow: America's Century of Regime Change from Hawaii to Iraq*
Charles C. Mann, *1491: New Revelations of the Americas before Columbus*
Calvin Luther Martin, *The Way of the Human Being*
Thomas Moore, *Dark Nights of the Soul*
Peter Nobakov, *Native American Testimony*
F. David Peat, *Blackfoot Physics: A Journey into the Native American Universe*
David Roediger, *The Wages of Whiteness: Race and the Making of the American Working Class*
Peter Silver, *Our Savage Neighbors: How Indian War Transformed Early America*
Philip Slater, *The Pursuit of Loneliness: American Culture at the Breaking Point*
Audrey Smedley, *Race in North America: Origins and Development of a Worldview*
Ronald Takaki, *Strangers from a Different Shore: A History of Asian Americans*
Robert M. Utley, *Indian Wars*
Robert M. Utley, *The Lance and the Shield: The Life and Times of Sitting Bull*
Dale Van Every, *Disinherited: The Lost Birthright of the American Indian*
Steven Waldman, *Founding Faith: Providence, Politics, and the Birth of Religious Freedom in America*
David Wellman, *Portraits of White Racism*
James Wilson, *The Earth Shall Weep: A History of Native America*
Howard Zinn, *A People's History of the United States*

Allan G. Johnson is a nationally recognized sociologist, nonfiction author, novelist, and public speaker best known for his work on issues of privilege and oppression, especially in relation to gender and race. He is the author of numerous books, including *The Gender Knot: Unraveling Our Patriarchal Legacy* and *The Forest and the Trees: Sociology as Life, Practice, and Promise* (both Temple) and *Privilege, Power, and Difference*. His work has been translated into several languages and excerpted in numerous anthologies. Visit him online at www.agjohnson.us and follow his blog at agjohnson.wordpress.com.